THE BEST OF AFRICAN COOKING

Over 130 Authentic African Recipes

First published by

Esanjam

P.O Box 1128

Luton, Bedfordshire LU1 1WT

www.esanjam.com

Email: info@esanjam.com

© Manjase Banda 2004

First published 2004

Revised Edition 2007

ISBN- 0-9546821-3-0

ISBN- 13 978-0-9546821-3-2

Author: Manjase Banda

Publisher: Esanjam

Project coordination: Esanjam

Book design and layout: Manjase Banda

Typeset in Book Antiqua

Contents

Introduction

African cooking, just like any other cuisine around the world, has a variety of interesting ingredients, which are explored in this book. Do not let the fact that African food has been left in the dark for so long put you off.

African Cooking: Africa has some of the most exciting and adventurous foods one can ever imagine. African food is healthy and most of the nutrients are contained in only one meal, because African cooking is mainly composed of mixing different foods together in one pan, such as the famous West African dish jollof rice.

Implements: Some of the instrument that are needed to cook African food include a mortar, a big heavy-based pan and a special wooden spoon used to make staple foods such as fufu, nshima and gari.

In Africa, different ingredients and ways of cooking are used. From the recipes in this book you will find that Africa has an extensive range of cuisines. From the north to the south, in central, eastern and western parts of Africa, people have mastered different ways of cooking and eating.

Some writers have tried to paint a very negative picture of African cooking. I can only blame ignorance. If these writers took the time to learn more about Africans and to take in the beauty of mother Africa they would experience what every person who lives and has lived in Africa has experienced the beauty and fantastic food.

Ingredients Used

Oils

Groundnut oil: This oil is made from peanuts and is extensively used in dishes from most parts of Africa. This oil is mostly used in frying and stews.

Ghee: This is a clarified butter, which melts into oil when heated. It gives an authentic nutty flavour when used in cuisines. Ghee is commonly used in most part of Africa.

Palm oil: This bright orange/red coloured 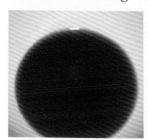 oil is extracted from palms and has a unique flavour and aroma. This oil is extensively used in African dishes and has an authentic flavour. There is no substitute for the taste you get from this oil.

Peanut paste: This is roasted peanut made into a paste; peanut butter can be used as a substitute for peanut paste if you can't get the real thing. However you can make the peanut  paste yourself, to get a real authentic taste.

Herbs And Spices

Parsley: This herb is used throughout Africa. It is used fresh or dried in soups and stews.

Coriander: In Africa fresh or dried coriander is used in stews and cold dishes. Coriander adds an intense flavour to meat and vegetable dishes.

Chillies: Chillies or hot peppers are now grown in most parts of Africa and are commonly used as seasoning, in fish and meat dishes, as well as in soups and stews. Chillies come in red, yellow, or brown.

Curry powder: Now also used extensively in most African cuisines.

Black pepper: Also used in most African soups and stew.

Tubers And Roots

 *Cassava:* This is a root which can be eaten fresh, dried or cooked. It has tough brown skin and a hard starchy white flesh. The skin needs to be peeled off before the root is used. When the cassava is dried and ground it can also be made into cassava

flour. Cassava leaves are also used in stews and soups in African cookery.

Gari: This is also made from roasted pounded cassava, often grainy in texture. Cassava is ground, fermented and roasted to make this coarse flour. Gari has a slightly sour taste which complements breads or African stiff porridge called gari.

Yam: The yam is a tuber that should not be confused with the sweet potato. Yams have an either yellow or white flesh; they can be eaten

baked, boiled, roasted, made into chips or pounded to make a stiff porridge. They come in different sizes. Although the yam is commonly used all around Africa, there are other varieties used in other parts of the world, such as the water yam, which as you might expect, is high in water content and is slimy to the touch. And the cocoyam, which has a white or pink hard outer harder shell, is often smaller.

Pounded yam: This is a yam that has been dried and pounded to make flour. The yam flour is used to make a stiff porridge as a substitute for the fresh variety.

Plantains: These are members of the banana family, though they are usually slightly larger. Plantains can be green, yellow or black in

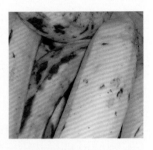

colour of ripeness, and all varieties can be used. Plantain can either be fried, or boiled as we see later.

Maize: This is like corn and is eaten fresh in most parts of Africa but used most extensively in most parts to make a stiff porridge. Samp, as shown here, is also made from dried cracked maize.

Couscous: Small grains of wheat rolled in flour, mostly eaten in the northern part of Africa.

Semolina: These are small grains of flour eaten in most parts of Africa. This is usually used to make porridge, puddings, and mixed with other flours to make very beautiful dishes.

Sorghum: This is often ground into flour to make cakes, porridge, African fermented drinks or mash.

Sweet potatoes: These come with a white or red skin and the flesh is either white or yellow. Sweet potatoes can be boiled, roasted, fried, creamed or baked, either in their skins or peeled.

They are easily combined with both sweet and savoury dishes. The sweet potato leaves that grow above the ground are also used in African cooking. They are usually added to stews and soups.

Lentils: Lentils are used all over the African continent, as in the rest of the world. They are most commonly soaked overnight, boiled and mashed together with other vegetables to be used as accompaniment to a meat or fish dish.

Millet: This is a small yellow grain with a mild, usually sweet flavour. The grain kernels are very small and round; are sometimes

ivory in colour, though some varieties are darker. This nutty and slightly bitter grain is made into a stiff porridge or used to make a large variety of other cuisines.

Vegetables And Fruits

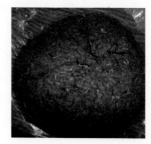

Cassava leaves: Are added to stews and can be purchased dried or fresh in African food stores. Here the cassava has already been processed.

Egusi: These are melon seeds, usually dried and ground before they are used in most soups. They have a nutty flavour, although pumpkin seeds can be used as a substitute. The egusi featured in this book was made from melon seeds.

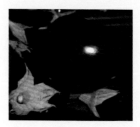

Eggplant/ Aubergine: Usually purple or yellow in colour. The purple variety is used in this book. Eggplant is used widely in most

7

parts of Africa. It is mixed into a variety of vegetable dishes, meat/fish dishes and sauces.

Garden egg: This is a member of the eggplant family, usually white or orange when ripe, and very small in size. These are often used in stews and soups.

Okra: This vegetable is green in colour and used in most African cooking. It is used in

stews and soups, or boiled and eaten on its own as a vegetable. To prepare the okra for cooking one needs to wash thoroughly, topping, tailing and cutting up.

Dried okra: Okra is usually dried and preserved to be used through out the year. Dried okra is used in most parts of Africa as a base for soups and stews.

Black-eyed beans: Also called cow peas, these are a staple of African cooking and are used in just about every type of dish from stews to starches to snacks like akara and moyi moyi.

Kidney beans: These are usually red in colour and are shaped like a kidney. They are used to make several dishes in Africa, including pasties, stews and cakes.

Spinach: In Africa the spinach is often chopped fresh and added into different kinds of soups, sauces and hot dishes. African spinach demands cooking.

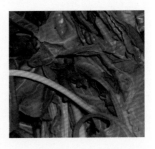

Pumpkin: This usually has a hard outer shell and yellow flesh, which is usually boiled until tender. In African cooking it is also used in soups and stews and the seed when dried can be dry-roasted and eaten or dried and ground then used in soup, stews or vegetable dishes. Along with other types of squash they are boiled, mashed, fried or used in sauces and rice. The pumpkin leaves are also eaten as a vegetable and are also added to stews and soups.

Bitter leaf: This is a bitter vegetable. It is green in colour and has a bitter taste. It needs to be cleaned appropriately, other wise it may make stews very bitter when  used. Only a small amount should be used in stews to add a very distinct, wonderful flavour. There is no substitute for this vegetable.

Hot peppers: Many different types, colours and sizes of hot pepper are available in West and Central Africa, but one thing they have in common is heat. If you like spicy  food, do not hold back here. In some parts of Africa peppers are used generously to make what can only be described as fiery dishes. Remove the veins and seeds to decrease the heat.

Mponda: This has a green outer shell and white flesh. Mponda is a member of the pumpkin family and is usually boiled and eaten  with honey or sugar and crushed peanuts or added to stews.

Lumanda: This is a wild vegetable found in most parts of Africa. It is green in colour and is used mostly in soups and stews. In most  parts of Zambia This vegetable is used to make a dish called Sashila/ifisashi. This is a traditional Zambian dish made with groundnuts and Vegetables. Usually wild vegetable such a lumanda are used but you can use other greens such as pumpkin leave, spinach and collard greens.

African mushroom: These are usually very tasty, and they come in different colours. In this book the orange variety were used.

Coconut: This has a very hard brown outer shell, white flesh and coconut water. The flesh and water from the coconut is widely used in African cuisines, alternatively you can drink the water, or use it to make a  drinks. The white flesh is often grated for cooking.

Avocado: These fruits can be either large or small and are shaped like pears; they are often referred to as avocado pears. They have dark green skin, a soft, light green, buttery flesh and an oval pit is in the centre of the fruit. They are used in salads, or cooking.

Bananas: These are also used extensively in African cooking and are also commonly eaten without preparation, mostly being served at the end of a meal. Green bananas are also used as a green vegetable; they are mostly boiled, with or without their skin.

Mangoes: These fruits are usually sweet and juicy and are either small or large. When ripened the small ones turn yellow and larger ones have green skin but yellow flesh. Mango trees are a common sight in many African countries. Although the peels are often eaten together with the flesh, it is best to peel the fruit before eating.

Papaya: This fruit is usually green but turns yellow when it ripens. The flesh also turns yellow and becomes slightly soft. It has dark seeds, which should be removed before you eat the fruit. To eat the fruit peel away the skin, remove the seeds and eat the sweet yellow flesh. This fruit, also known as paw-paw, comes in a range of sizes and is round.

Guava: This round fruit has a thin green or yellow skin and pink or white flesh, which is sweet. The centre has tiny seeds, which are also eaten.

Tamarind- The tamarind is an evergreen tree found in most parts of Africa. The tamarind fruit is a seed pod, brown in colour and several inches long, containing a sour or sweet tasting or pulp, which can be used in cooking or eaten as a fruit.

Fish and Caterpillars

Kapenta: These are small fish, they look like sardines, and are eaten when fresh and also dried. They are used in most stews and soups.

Vinkwala/ Mopani worms: These are large caterpillars. They are an important source of protein in African meals. They are hand  picked, prepared, dried and stored. They are usually fried or roasted.

Crawfish: these have a hard outer shell and they come in several colours, white, yellow, red or dark brown. They are widely used in west African cuisine.

Northern Africa

Northern Africa has some of the most exiting cuisines. Ingredients such as cous cous, lentils, dates, herbs, cashew nuts and chickpeas are used to make wonderful stews, dips and deserts unique to this region.

Grilled Chicken With A Chilli Paste (Tunisia)

Chilli Paste
1 cup dried red chillies
1 cup olive oil
5 garlic cloves,
2 cups fresh coriander
Salt to taste

Chicken
500g chicken breast cut into bite size pieces
1 small onion grated
1 tsp ground cumin
½ cup chopped Parsley
Juice of one lemon
2 courgettes chopped

1 Cut each chilli in half and remove the seed by shaking the chilli once you have removed most of the seeds. Soak the chillies in hot water for 1 hour. Drain and put the chillies, garlic, olive oil and the fresh coriander in the blender and blend until you have a smooth mixture, then add salt to taste. Put this mixture in a jar and top with some olive oil. Whenever the paste is used, make sure to top with olive oil to stop from spoiling.

2 To make the marinade for the chicken, blend or pound in mortar 3 tablespoons of the chilli paste and 3 tablespoons of olive oil, parsley, cumin, grated onion and the juice of one lemon. Cut the chicken into bite-size pieces and add to the marinade. Massage the marinade into the chicken with your hands, then cover and leave to marinate for 2 hours. Place the chicken and courgettes on skewers, starting with a piece of chicken followed by a courgette, until the skewer is full. Grill or griddle the chicken, turning until it is evenly browned on all sides. Serve with flat bread.

Tip: Wash hands, pat dry then oil the hand with a little olive oil before you start handling the chillies. After handing chillies always wash your hands thoroughly with plenty of soap and water.

Vegetables Baked In A Herb Marinate

1 large aubergine
1 large onion
2 large potatoes
2 courgettes
Salt to taste

Herb Marinate:
1 cups fresh coriander
5 garlic cloves
3 small fresh red chilli
½ cup fresh parsley
½ cup olive oil

1 Start by washing the potatoes, aubergine and courgettes and slicing into thin disks. Peel the onion and cut into discs. Put all the ingredients in a large dish filled with water and 1 tablespoon of salt. Leave the vegetables for 30 minutes

2 Put the fresh coriander, garlic, chilli, parsley olive oil and salt to taste in a blender and blend to a smooth mixture. Drain the vegetable and marinade with the herb marinade for another 30 minutes. Put the vegetable and marinade in a baking dish, cover with foil and roast in preheated oven on gas mark 4 (180°C) until the potatoes are tender – about 35 minutes.

Serve this dish as a main meal.

Carrot Salad

4 carrots
Juice of 2 lemons
4 tbsp honey
2 tbsp syrup

1 Peel and grate the carrots and put in a bowl. Squeeze the lemons in another bowl and add the honey and syrup and mix thoroughly. Add the lemon mixture to the carrots and mix well. Serve as a salad with a meat dish.

Note: *You can substitute lemon juice for orange juice.*

Chickpeas Balls (Egypt)

800g chickpeas
1 tbsp Black pepper
1 tsp ground cumin
2 tbsp coarse semolina
½ cup fresh coriander
1 tbsp baking soda
1 small onion grated
3 tbsp olive oil
Salt to taste

1 Soak the chickpeas overnight; drain and rinse, using cold water. Boil the chickpeas until they are tender. Drain the chickpeas and put them in a food processor or mortar. Pound/process the chickpeas to get a grainy texture. Add the grated onions, finely chopped coriander, cumin, semolina, baking soda and salt.

2 Taking about 1 tablespoon of the mixture at a time, form into balls. Let the balls set another 15 minutes. Grease a baking tray with the a generous amount of olive oil, then put the patties on the baking tray and bake in a preheated oven at gas mark 5 (190°C) for about 30-35 minutes.

Serve with fresh bread, some mustard, tomato sauce and a salad.

Fish In Tahini And Lemon Sauce (Egypt)

1 fresh tilapia fish
3 tbsp tahini
1 lemon
1 small chilli
1 small onion
2 garlic cloves crushed
3 tbsp olive oil
Salt to taste

1 Make the marinade with the tahini, crushed garlic and salt. Put the fish in the tahini marinade and leave for 30 minutes. Put the olive oil in a large pan, add the fish and shallow fry on each side for 3 minutes.

2 Put the fried fish and the chopped onions in a baking dish along with the tahini marinade and cover with foil, then bake in a preheated oven at gas mark 4 (180°C) for 30 minutes.

Serve with a slice of lemon and a salad, or with roasted potatoes.

Hummus (Egypt)

Hummus is a paste commonly eaten in the Egypt. It is made from check peas.

500g chickpeas, soaked overnight
6 garlic cloves, crushed
4 tbsp tahini
1 tsp paprika
1 tsp salt
4 tbsp olive oil to serve
5 tbsp water
¾ cup chopped parsley
Juice of one large lemon

1 Drain the chickpeas and put in a pan with enough water to cover, bring to the boil, then simmer for 1½ hours or until the chickpeas are tender. Add more water if needed. Do not add salt while simmering, as this will make the chickpeas very tough. Once chickpeas are tender drain and set aside.

2 Place the chickpeas with the tahini, crushed garlic, parsley and the lemon juice in a blender or mortar if you have one and blend or pound to a smooth paste and then add salt and mix thoroughly. Serve with some crusty bread and a salad or roasted meat.

Tip: *When serving, put the hummus in bowl with a drizzle of olive oil and dusting of cayenne pepper.*

Kosheri, (Egypt)

1 cup lentils
1 cup chickpeas
1½ cups any pasta
70ml olive oil
1 tbsp crushed garlic
2 tbsp tomato paste
2 large fresh tomatoes, chopped
1 red bell pepper
¼ cup chopped parsley
1 green chilli, chopped
Juice of a lemon
1 large onion, chopped
Salt to taste

This is a simple dish made with lentils, pasta, chickpeas and tomato sauce.

1 Soak the chickpeas overnight, then drain and put in a large pan with enough water to cover and bring to the boil. Simmer for 1½ hours or until the chickpeas are tender, then set aside. Put the pasta in a large pan filled with boiling water and cook for 10-15 minutes or until tender. Drain and set aside. Rinse the lentils and put in a large saucepan filled with water, bring to the boil and simmer for 30-35 minutes or until they are tender, drain and set aside.

2 To make the sauce, first saute the chopped onion, bell pepper and crushed garlic in olive oil until the onions are transparent. Add the chopped tomatoes and tomato paste, and then simmer for 20 minutes. Add the pasta, lentils, chickpeas and chopped parsley and mix. Remove from heat immediately and add salt and lemon juice and mix. Finally, slice onion in thin, pieces and saute in 1 tablespoon oil until brown and crispy. Serve the dish while hot with the crisp fried onions on top.

Tip: You can also add any meat to this dish such as fried chicken cut into bite-size piece.

Prawns And Couscous (Morocco)

The combination of couscous and prawns in a coconut sauce works well.

700g fresh prawns in their shells
1 large onion
2 apples peeled cored and chopped into cubes
1 large red pepper
2 tbsp cashew nuts
2 fresh tomatoes chopped
350ml coconut milk
2 tbsp fresh parsley chopped
3 garlic cloves crushed
¼ cup chopped parsley
2 tablespoons black pepper
1 chilli
Salt to taste
Olive oil
Juice of 1 lemon

1 Heat 3 tablespoons of oil in a heavy saucepan and fry about a half of the onion rings until they are golden brown. Transfer to a plate. Put the apples in the same pan and fry until they are light brown, transfer to plate with the onion rings. Add the cashew nuts and fry until they are golden brown. Add to the plate with the onions and apples and set aside.

2 Heat 5 tablespoons of olive oil in the same pan and add the rest of the onion, fry until the onion is golden brown, add the peppers and garlic and cook until peppers are soft, stirring occasionally. Add the fresh tomatoes, tomato paste and coconut milk and reduce the heat and simmer for 20 minutes. Clean and wash the prawn and remove the shells. Add the prawns to the pan and simmer for a further 10 minutes. Season with salt and pepper and finish with freshly squeezed lemon juice. Prepare the couscous by putting it in a large bowl with enough boiling stock just to cover the couscous, then cover and leave the couscous to absorb all the liquid (or prepare couscous according to the instructions on the packet). Add the chopped parsley and mix. Serve the couscous with a topping of the prawns, fried onions, apples and cashew nuts.

Minced Lamb with Vegetables (Sudan)

2 small bell peppers or 1 large one
1 large aubergine sliced into cubes
2 large potatoes peeled and chopped
in small cubes
450g minced lamb
2 large fresh tomatoes
Flour for dusting
2 tbsp fresh sage chopped
1 large onion chopped
1 tbsp tomato past
1 tsp sugar
1 tbsp curry powder
1 tbsp chilli powder
3 courgettes
2 large fresh tomatoes
100ml vegetable stock
70ml olive oil
Vegetable oil
2 garlic cloves crushed
Salt to taste

This recipe is interesting because of the contrast of the aubergine and the courgettes.

1 Slice the aubergines, dust with salt and leave for 30 minutes. Cut courgettes and potato and sprinkle with salt. Dust all the vegetables with flour. Heat oil in a heavy-based pan and fry all the vegetables in batches until golden brown, then set aside.

2 Put the 70ml olive oil, the onion and chopped bell peppers in a pan and fry until the onions are transparent. Add the minced lamb, crushed garlic, curry powder, chilli powder and sugar and cook for 20 minutes or until the meat is evenly browned. Add the fresh tomatoes, tomato paste, and coriander and simmer until the tomatoes are tender. Add the broth and simmer for 20 minutes.

Serve the vegetables on a plate with minced lamb stew on top with some flat bread.

Sudanese Salad

2 fresh tomatoes,
2 cucumbers
1 small onion
½ red pepper
½ cup lime juice
1 small onion
6 leaves lettuce
50 ml olive oil
Handful fresh parsley,
chopped
Stoned olives, chopped

1 Finely chop the tomatoes, onions and pepper and put in large bowl. Add the chopped olives, then peel the cucumbers and chop into cubes and add to the bowl.

2 Mix the lime juice with the olive oil and add the chopped parsley then pour over the salad and mix until all the ingredients are well coated.

Serve as a side salad.

A Vegetable Dish (Libya)

1 large eggplant
2 tomatoes
1 courgette
1 tbsp tomato paste
1 large potato, cubed
½ cup stoned olives
4 fresh jalapeno peppers chopped
¼ tsp chilli pepper
4 garlic cloves crushed
¼ cup fresh coriander chopped
1 small onion
Olive oil
5 pickled green jalapeno peppers chopped
650ml water
Salt
Vegetable oil for frying

1 Start by cutting the eggplant into cubes and putting in a large bowl filled with 600ml water and one tablespoon of salt. Leave for 30 minutes, then drain. Meanwhile chop the courgettes and potato into cubes. Deep-fry the courgettes, eggplant and the potato in the vegetable oil separately until they are golden brown. Pile on a greaseproof paper to remove excess oil.

2 Put 6 tablespoons of olive oil in a pan, add the onion and fry until it is transparent. Add the cumin, garlic, fresh tomatoes, tomato paste and simmer on low heat for 20 minutes or until the tomatoes are cooked. Add the stoned olives, the jalapenos and 50ml water, then simmer for 15 minutes. Serve the vegetables on a plate with some pouring sauce on top and a sprinkle of coriander.

Lamb, Vegetables And Couscous (Morocco)

450g lamb mince
1 onion
1 small bunch of coriander
1 small bunch of parsley
300g pumpkin, seeded, peeled and cut into chunks
300g carrots peeled and cut into chunks
300g aubergines cut into thick chunks
5 okra (lady fingers)
½ large green pepper
1 tsp black pepper
30ml olive oil
2 cups couscous
½ cup cooked chickpeas
1 stock cube
1 tsp cumin
1 tsp ground coriander
1 tsp turmeric
2 tbsp tomato paste
1 tsp salt
200ml vegetable stock

1 Heat a large heavy-based pan, add the stock and the lamb and bring to the boil. Add the oil, black pepper, turmeric, cumin, fresh ginger, and a sprig of parsley and coriander tied together. Cover and simmer for 45 minutes. Add the tomatoes, onion and carrots and simmer for another 30 minutes. Then add the courgettes, okra, pumpkin, aubergine, peppers and salt and simmer for a further 30 minutes.

2 Place couscous in a large bowl with stock cube and enough hot water to cover and leave until the couscous absorbs all the liquid. Or prepare according to the instructions on the packet. Once the couscous is ready, add the cooked chickpeas and mix thoroughly. Serve the couscous hot when ready by making a little well in the centre of the couscous and placing the vegetable, lamb and some broth in it.

Note: The vegetables used can change from season to season and you can use any vegetables you like. This recipe has a combination of vegetables that I have tried and think work well.

Meat Pastries (Egypt)

Dough
800g flour
2 tsp salt
1½ tbsp fast raising yeast
2 tsp baking powder
2 tbsp powdered milk
1 tbsp sugar
100ml olive oil
440ml water

Meat filling
400g. Minced lamb
300g. Chicken meat minced
1 medium onion
5 garlic cloves
5 large carrots grated
100ml olive oil
1-cup fresh chopped coriander
2 tsp curry powder
4 tsp black pepper
1 medium potato finely chopped
1 small fresh red chilli
Water

1 Sift the flour, salt, baking powder and milk into a bowl. Add the sugar and olive oil and rub in, to get a mixture that resembles fine breadcrumbs. Add the yeast and mix, then add the water and mix to make a non-stick dough.

2 Knead the dough on a flat surface for 20 minutes. Put the dough in a well-oiled bowl, cover and keep in a warm place for the dough to rise – about 6 hours. Once the dough has doubled in size, knead again for 10 minutes then put the dough back in the bowl and leave the dough covered in a warm place for about 30 minutes.

3 Meanwhile, prepare the filling for the dough. Put the olive oil in a pan and add the chopped onion, crushed garlic and cook until the onion is transparent. Add the chopped coriander, grated carrots, curry powder, black pepper and cook on very low heat for 10 minutes. Add the minced lamb and 6 tablespoons water and simmer for 15 minutes, then add the minced chicken, chopped chilli, 6 tablespoon water and salt and cook for a further 10 minutes. Finally add the peeled and finely chopped potato, 4 tablespoons olive oil and simmer for 30 minutes.

4 Allow the filling to cool, and then divide the dough into two, roll out one half of the dough thinly and cut into round circles using a small round plate, about 15 cm, 6 inches in diameter. Put a generous amount of the filling on one side of the pastry, brush the edges of the pastry with water and fold over the circle to make the pastries. Repeat this with rest of the dough and the filling. Bake in preheated oven on gas mark 4 (180°C) for 30-35 minutes or until golden brown.

Note: You can fry these pastries or roll out the dough as thinly or thickly as you like; or make the pastries smaller, larger or any shape you want.

Roasted Eggplant

2 large eggplants
1 red bell pepper
1 green chilli finely chopped
4 tbsp olive oil
3 tbsp lemon juice
2 cloves garlic crushed
3 tbsp fresh coriander chopped
1 spring onion finely chopped
Salt to taste

1 Prepare the eggplant and peppers by rubbing them with olive oil, then wrapping each ingredient separately in foil. Place the wrapped ingredients on a baking sheet and bake in a preheated oven gas mark 4 (180°C) for 30 to 35 minutes or until tender. Once cooked leave to cool, then cut of the stalk and peel the eggplant. Chop roughly, and transfer to a bowl.

2 Finely chop the bell pepper and add to the eggplant, then add the crushed garlic, spring onion, chilli, coriander, lemon juice, olive oil and salt, mix thoroughly.

Serve warm or cold with flat bread

Date Tart

Dough
50g flour
200g coarse semolina
6 heaped tbsp butter melted
1 tsp baking powder
200ml warm water
6 tbsp sugar

Date paste
310g whole stoned dates
½ cup flaked almonds
200ml water
1 tsp ground nutmeg

1 Mix semolina, flour, sugar and baking powder in a bowl, add the butter and mix, add the warm water to make a soft but non-sticky dough. Knead the dough until it is soft and smooth. Cover the dough and leave it in the fridge for 30 minutes. Put the pastry in baking dish and spread out with your fingers to all corners. Blind bake the pastry in a preheated oven at gas mark 5 (190°C) for 20 minutes. Once ready leave to cool.

2 Meanwhile make the date filling by blending the dates with water to make a smooth paste, add nutmeg, ginger to the dates and mix thoroughly. Fill the tart with the date filling and arrange the flaked almonds on top then bake the pastry in a preheated oven at gas mark 3 (160°C) for 20 minutes or until the almonds are golden brown. Leave to cool and serve as a desert.

Almond Biscuit (Libya)

100g icing sugar
150g flour
4 tbsp butter or ghee
100g ground Almond
1 tsp almond essence
3 tbsp water

1 Melt the butter in a large saucepan, then add the sugar and almond essence and mix. In a large bowl mix the ground almonds and flour, add the butter mixture and rub in, add the water and mix the mixture together.

2 The mixture should be crumbly, gather the mixture together and put in a greased baking tin. Spread the mixture to the edges of the tin and Press down until the surface is even. Cut the dough into rectangular shapes in the baking tin and bake in a preheated oven at gas mark 4 (180°C) for 30 minutes or until the biscuit is golden brown.

Serve as a snack or with tea.

Sudanese Cake

This is a desert made from semolina and yoghurt, served with a thick syrup and yoghurt.

100g sugar
50g unsalted butter
or ghee
2 tablespoon roasted
whole almonds
½ cup yoghurt
1 tsp baking powder
100g coarse semolina

Syrup
Juice of 1 lemon
4 tbsp icing sugar
4 tbsp honey
100ml water

1 Beat the yoghurt and the sugar in a large mixing bowl. Add melted butter and semolina and beat until the mixture is well mixed. Pour the mixture in a small buttered loaf tin and bake in a preheated oven at gas mark 4 (180°C) for 25-30 minutes or until the cake is golden brown.

2 To make the thick syrup put the icing sugar, water, honey and lemon juice in a sauce pan and bring to the boil, simmering until it thickens. Set aside to cool. Pour the cold syrup over the desert, toast the almonds until golden brown, crush slightly and sprinkle on top of dessert. Serve with yoghurt.

Date Pastries Libya

Dough
50g flour
100g fine semolina
100g coarse semolina
6 heaped tbsp butter melted
1 tsp baking powder
100ml water
1½ cups warm water

Date paste
200g whole stoned dates
4 tbsp water
1 tsp nutmeg
1 tsp ground ginger
2 tsp vegetable oil

Sugar syrup
4 tbsp sugar
100ml water
2 tbsp honey
3 tbsp sesame seeds

1 Mix semolina, flour and baking powder in a bowl, add the butter and mix. Add the warm water to make a soft but non-sticky dough. Take a handful of the mixture, and try to roll it; if it crumbles you need to add a little more water. Knead the dough until it is soft and smooth. Cover the dough and leave it in the fridge for 30 minutes. Meanwhile make the date filling by blending the dates, water and oil to make a smooth paste, add the nutmeg and ginger and mix thoroughly.

2 Remove the dough from the fridge and roll out on a flat surface. Spread the date paste on the dough, then roll the dough into a swiss roll (it should look like a sausage), then flatten slightly. Cut the dough diagonally into 1½ inch pieces. Arrange on a baking sheet. Bake in a preheated oven at gas mark 4 (180°C) for 25-35 minutes, or until golden brown. Make a sugar and honey syrup mixture by dissolving the sugar in the water, add the honey and boil until the syrup is light brown. Pour over the pastries while still hot and garnish with sesame seeds.

Coconut Desert

450g coconut cream
7 tbsp sugar
8 tbsp grated coconut
1 tsp ground cardamom

1 Mix the coconut cream and sugar in a saucepan and heat for 5 minutes. Add the grated coconut and cardamom and simmer until the mixture starts to thicken, stirring from time to time to stop the mixture from sticking to the pan.

2 Once all the liquid has evaporated, transfer the mixture to a greased baking dish. Bake in a preheated oven at gas mark 4 (180°C) for 25 minutes or until the sides turn light brown. Remove from oven, cool the desert, then cut into cubes and serve as a snack or desert.

Chicken Stew (Egypt)

1 whole chicken quartered
Juice of 1 lemon
1 large onion
1 tbsp cumin powder
2 large tomatoes
1 tbsp tomato paste
½ cup stoned olives
70ml olive oil
2 carrots peeled and finely
chopped
10 lady fingers (okra)
3 garlic cloves crushed
1 cup chickpeas soaked over
night (or canned chickpeas)
5 green cardamom seeds
150 ml water

1 Drain the chickpeas, put them in a pan and add enough water to cover. Simmer for 1½-2 hours or until the chickpeas are tender, then put aside for use later in the recipe. Put the olive oil in another large heavy-based pan and fry the chicken for 10 minutes, then add the cumin, crushed garlic and fry for a further 10 minutes.

2 Put the onion, fresh tomatoes and tomato paste in a blender and blend to a fine puree, add the puree to the chicken then add the 150ml water, cardamom seed, okra and carrots and simmer on very low heat for 20 minutes. Add the cooked chickpeas, and simmer for a further 20 minutes. Finally add the stoned olives and the lemon juice and serve with boiled rice or cous cous.

Southern Africa

Southern African cuisine is exiting and adventurous. Ingredients such as peanuts, maize, corn, dry vegetables, wild mushrooms and dry meat are used to make tasty dishes that will leave you wanting more.

Prawns And Vegetables (Mozambique)

1 large onion, chopped
2 large tomatoes, chopped
1 tbsp tomato paste
½ red bell pepper, chopped
1½ cups fresh prawns in their shells
2 tbsp vegetable oil
1 red chilli chopped
1 vegetable stock cube
3 cups fresh pumpkin leaves chopped
3 tbsp smooth peanut butter
250ml water
Salt to taste

This recipe combines prawns, peanut butter and fresh greens.

1 Wash pumpkin leaves thoroughly, making sure to wash off all earth. Roll the pumpkin leaves into a bundle, cut the vegetables into thin strips, then put into a large heavy-based pan along with 100ml of water and the stock cube and cook for 10 minutes. Add chopped tomatoes, vegetable oil, bell pepper, and tomato paste and simmer until the tomatoes are tender – for about 20 minutes.

2 Add another 100ml of water and the peanut butter (do not stir at this point), simmer for another 10 minutes. Finally, remove the prawns from their shells and add to the pan, along with the chilli and 50ml water. Stir, then simmer for a further 10 minutes, stirring occasionally to avoid burning. Serve with nshima.

Note: *You can use collard greens or spinach in place of the pumpkin leaves.*

Chicken And Beans Stew (Swaziland)

400g chicken chopped or a medium chicken
200g broad beans
4 garlic cloves
70ml olive oil or vegetable oil
1 tsp curry powder
1 tsp paprika
1 onion
2 fresh tomatoes
1 green pepper
1 vegetable stock cube
2 cups water

1 Put the beans in a large pan with enough water to cover. Bring to the boil, then simmer the beans for 45 minutes or until they are tender, then set aside. In another pan put the chicken, stock cube, curry powder, black pepper, paprika, and 2 cups water and cook for 20 minutes. Remove the chicken from the broth and set aside. Do not discard the broth, as it will be needed for later use.

2 In another pan fry the onion, garlic and green peppers in the olive oil until the onions are transparent. Add the chicken and continue frying on low heat for 10 minutes. Add the chopped tomatoes and cook until the tomatoes are tender Add the broad beans and the broth and simmer for 20 minutes. Serve hot with nshima.

Note: *Kidney beans and black eye peas also work well in this dish, but you will need to make sure you boil the beans until they are tender. Some beans may need to be boiled longer; it depends on the type of bean.*

Smoked Dried Meat Stew (South Africa)

500g smoked dried meat
3 sausages chopped
2 large onions
3 large tomatoes
1 bell pepper
2 large potatoes
70ml vegetable oil
1 vegetable stock cube
600ml water
Salt to taste

1 Wash the meat in cold water to remove smoky taste. Heat the vegetable oil in a large pan, add the onion and fry for 5 minutes, then add the blended tomatoes and bell pepper and cook for a further 5 minutes. Cut the meat into small pieces and add to the sauce, add the water, vegetable stock and simmer for 2 hours, adding more water when needed.

2 Add the salt and the peeled and chopped potatoes and the chopped sausage and simmer for a further 30 minutes or until the potatoes are tender. Serve hot with nshima/sadza.

Chicken Stew (Zambia)

1.4kg free-range chicken
1 large onion
2 large fresh tomatoes
4 cups water
Salt to taste
70ml vegetable oil

This is a very old but simple recipe which was passed on to me by my grandmother.

1 Put the chopped onions and the oil in a large heavy-based pan and fry the onions until they are golden brown then set aside. Do not burn the onions because this will give the chicken a bitter taste.

2 Clean the chicken and cut into pieces. Add the chicken pieces and salt to the pan with the fried onions and mix. Add the two cups of water and cook on low heat until all the water has reduced to oil (about 30-35 minutes).

3 Reduce the heat and fry the chicken on very low heat for 10 minutes or until the chicken is golden brown. Add the chopped tomatoes but do not mix. Cover the chicken and simmer until the tomatoes are cooked. Once the tomatoes are cooked add 2 cups water and simmer for a further 45 minutes or until chicken is tender. Serve with nshima and sashila, or plain rice.

Tip: *It is very important to use a whole free-range chicken in this recipe. Use the gizzard, chicken liver and chicken feet for extra flavour. It is advisable to get a chicken that has been reared on a farm and has been fed organic food.*

Seswaa With Onion (Botswana)

400g beef
1 cup fresh spinach
1 garlic clove, crushed
1 cup fresh cream
1 large onion
1 stock cube
Salt to taste
600ml water

Seswaa is pounded meat and is a traditional way of cooking meat in Botswana. This is a simple but tasty recipe, which requires patience, as it is a very slow cooking process. My version is slightly modified.

1 In a large heavy-based pan fry the onion until golden brown, then add the garlic, beef and the stock cube and enough water to cover the meat. Bring to the boil. Simmer the meat for one hour, then remove the beef from the pan. Put the beef into a mortar and separate the fibres by pounding. If you don't have a mortar you can use a food processor.

2 Meanwhile, clean the spinach and soak in hot water for 30 minutes. Drain, then blend to a puree. Transfer the meat back to the pan, add the spinach and black pepper, then simmer for a further 10 minutes. Add the fresh cream and serve hot with some warm bread.

Chicken And Okra (Zambia)

4 chicken breasts
100g okra
¼ cup fresh peas
1 large carrot peeled and
finely chopped
2 large fresh tomatoes
2 large onions
1 clove garlic
50g oz. butter
50ml oil
½ cup tomato ketchup
4 tbsp Worcestershire sauce
4 tbsp vinegar
1 large green pepper
1 tsp black pepper
250ml water

1 Cut the chicken breast into bite-size pieces and set aside. Put oil, butter, garlic green pepper and onion in the pan and fry until the pepper and onion become tender.

2 Add the chicken and continue cooking for 20 minutes. Add the diced fresh tomato and simmer for another 10 minutes or until the tomatoes become tender. Add the tomato ketchup, Worcestershire sauce, vinegar, okra, peas, carrot, salt and water and simmer for 30 minutes.

This can be served with the combination of the boiled baked sweet potatoes and white rice.

Beans In Tomato Sauce (Zambia)

200g kidney beans
1 tsp curry powder
1 tsp chilli powder
3 large tomatoes
2 tbsp tomato paste
1 tbsp sugar
1 large onion
70ml vegetable oil
Water

1 Wash the beans and soak overnight. Drain the water from the beans and transfer the beans to a large pan and add enough water to cover beans. Boil for 30 minutes.

2 Add oil, chopped tomatoes, onions, curry powder, tomato paste, sugar and more water to cover beans, then simmer for 2 hours, adding water if needed. Boil until the water has reduced. The beans should be tender and the sauce should be thick.

Serve with nshima or crusty bread.

Sashila (Pumpkin Leaves With Groundnuts)

(Zambia, Malawi, Botswana)

2 cups chopped pumpkin
leaves
1 small tomato, diced
1 small onion, chopped
5 heaped tbsp ground
peanuts
1 small chilli
1 tbsp vegetable oil
1 tsp baking soda
1½ cups water

1 Heat the water in a pan and add the soda, then add the washed and chopped pumpkin leaves and allow to cook on a low heat for 20 minutes, stirring from time to time to avoid the liquid boiling over.

2 Add the peanuts and stir thoroughly, then simmer for 10 minutes. Add the chopped tomatoes, onion, vegetable oil, the chopped chilli and simmer for a further 20 minutes, stirring from time to time to avoid the vegetable from burning. Serve with nshima and any meat stew.

Note: Collard greens or spinach can be used in place of pumpkin leaves.

African Mushrooms

2 cups African red mushroom
1 small onion chopped
1 large tomato chopped
1 tsp black pepper
70ml groundnut oil
Salt to taste

1 Clean the mushroom in plenty of water making sure to remove all the sand. Heat a heavy based pan and add the oil and the mushroom and cook for 5 minutes. Add the chopped onions and cook until the onions are transparent, add the tomato and salt, then simmer for 15 – 20 minutes. Serve with nshima.

Roasted Chicken Feet

4 chicken feet
1 tsp chilli powder
½ tsp black pepper
½ tsp curry powder
2 tbsp groundnut oil
½ tsp salt

1 Clean the chicken feet with plenty of water. Put in a bowl and add the groundnut oil, salt , curry powder, black pepper and chilli powder, massage the ingredients into the feet. Cover and leave to marinate for 10 – 15 minutes. Transfer the chicken feet to a greased baking tray. Roast in a preheated oven gas mark 4 (180ºC) for 25 -30 minutes. Serve as a snack.

Corn Meal Nshima With Sour Milk

800g corn meal
300ml water
600ml milk
Sour milk or Yoghurt
Sugar to taste

1 Put 600ml of the milk in a pot and heat until the milk starts to boil. Mix the 300ml of water with the 200g of corn meal in a bowl, add this mixture to the boiling milk stirring continuously until the mixture becomes porridge. Simmer the porridge for 20 minutes.

2 Add the rest of the corn meal stirring continuously until it becomes a stiff porridge. Scoop a portion of the nshima with a wooden spoon into a dip serving bowl and add enough sour milk or yoghurt to cover, add sugar to your taste and serve. Serve as a snack or main meal.

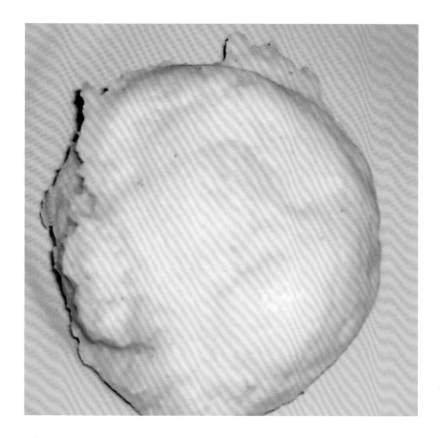

Nshima/Sadza (Zambia And Zimbabwe)

800g maize meal
900ml water

1 Put 600ml of the water in a pan and heat until the water starts to boil. Mix the other 300ml of the water with the 200g of maize meal in a bowl. Add this mixture to the boiling water, stirring continuously until the mixture becomes porridge. Simmer the porridge for 20 minutes.

2 Add the rest of the maize meal, stirring continuously until it becomes a stiff porridge. Serve with a meat or vegetable dish.

Note: *A special wooden spoon used for cooking African stiff porridge is best for this dish, but if you can't find one use any wooden spoon.*

Fish Baked With Green Bananas (Zambia)

2 fresh buga buga fish or trout
1 cup water
⅔ cup vinegar
1 tbsp. sugar
50g butter
2 tbsp vegetable oil
2 tbsp dried parsley
1 garlic clove, crushed
2 green bananas
3 medium fresh tomatoes
2 tbsp tomato paste
1 tsp salt
2 large sliced onions
1 green bell pepper
2 tsp black pepper

1 Clean the fish, put it in baking dish and set aside. Heat the vegetable oil in a saucepan. Add the butter, green pepper, onion, and crushed garlic and fry until the onion becomes tender.

2 Add the chopped tomatoes and simmer for 10 minutes, then add tomato paste, black pepper, sugar, salt, water and vinegar and stir thoroughly. Simmer for another 10 minutes.

3 Meanwhile peel the green bananas, slice into thin discs and add these to the baking dish. Then pour the hot sauce over the fish and bananas, sprinkle with parsley, cover with foil and bake for 45 minutes in a preheated oven at gas mark 4 (180°C) for 35 minutes. Serve with boiled rice.

Sweet Potatoes Stew

200g sweet potatoes peeled
and cut into cubes
6 tbsp vegetable oil
2 large fresh tomatoes
chopped
1 tsp black pepper
1 onion chopped
1 tbsp tomato paste
300ml water
Salt to taste

1 Heat the oil in a large heavy-based pan, add the chopped onion and garlic and fry until the onions are transparent about 5 minutes. Add the chopped tomatoes, tomato paste and black pepper, and simmer until the tomatoes are soft – about 10 minutes.

2 Add the sweet potatoes to the pan with the water, and enough salt to taste. Simmer on very low heat for 35-40 minutes or until the sweet potatoes are tender but not mushy. Serve as a side dish or as a main meal with a meat dish.

Maize Meal Dumplings

800g maize flour
550g flour
1½ tbsp fast rising yeast
100g sugar
1 tsp salt
900ml water

1 Put 600ml of the water in a pan and heat until the water starts to boil. Mix the other 300ml of the water and the 200g of maize meal in a bowl, add this mixture to the boiling water, stirring continuously until the mixture becomes a porridge. Simmer the porridge for 20 minutes, then add the rest of the maize meal and stir until it becomes a very stiff porridge. Set the stiff porridge aside to cool. Meanwhile, mix the flour, sugar, salt and the fast raising yeast.

2 Once the stiff porridge is cool, add the flour and the yeast mixture and knead to make a soft, non-sticky dough. Grease a bowl with oil, put the dough in the bowl, cover, put in a warm place and leave to rise for 1½-2 hours. When the dough has risen, roll into balls, small enough to fit in one hand. Steam the balls for 20-25 minutes. Test balls with knife by piercing centre. If the knife comes out clean then the balls are ready. Serve with meat, fish or chicken dish in this book.

Sweet Potato Balls

5 beef sausages
2 cups grated sweet potatoes
1 large onion grated
1 tsp coriander
1 tsp cumin
¼ cup fresh coriander
1 small green chilli
2 garlic cloves crushed
Oil for deep-frying
Salt to taste

1 Start by removing the sausages from their skins and place in a large bowl, add the grated sweet potatoes and onion to the sausage meat. Mix thoroughly. Add the cumin, salt, coriander, chopped chilli and crushed garlic, and mix.

2 Take a handful of the mixture and shape into small round balls; deep-fry the balls until they are golden brown. To finish cooking the sweet potato balls you need to put them on a large, well-greased baking tray and put in a preheated oven at gas mark 4 (180°C) for 20 minutes. Serve hot or cold with a salad or as a starter.

Note: *Any sausage meat can be used in this recipe.*

Soya Patties
(Zambia)

160g soya mince
1 large onion, chopped
¼ cup chopped coriander
1 tsp cumin
1 tsp garamasala
1 tsp salt
2 garlic cloves crushed
3 eggs
¼ cup fresh chopped parsley
Vegetable oil for deep-frying
3 tbsp milk

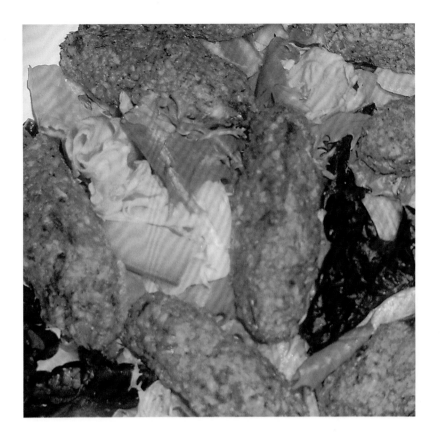

1 Put the soya mince in a bowl and add salt. Mix the eggs and milk in another bowl. Make a well in the centre of the mince, add the egg and milk mixture and mix until it becomes fluffy. Add the chopped onions, cumin, parsley, garamasala, and coriander and mix thoroughly.

2 Using your hands, shape the patties into any shape you want, heat the oil in a large pan then deep fry the patties a few at a time until they become golden brown. Put the patties on tray to cool, then serve with a salad.

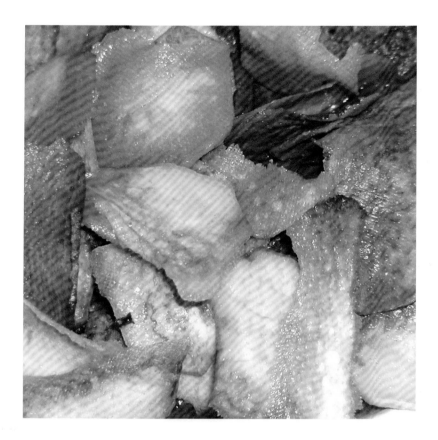

Sweet Potatoes Chips

2 large sweet potatoes
Salt to taste
1 tsp chilli powder
(optional)
Vegetable oil to frying

1 Wash the sweet potatoes, slice them into thin discs. Pat dry and set aside. Heat the oil in a large pan and deep-fry the sweet potatoes until they are golden brown.

2 Put the fried sweet potatoes on a serving dish. Add salt and chilli powder to taste, then serve with any meat dish.

Sweet Corn Savoury Scorns

250g fresh sweetcorn
kernels
2 tbsp plain flour
4 tbsp sorghum flour
1 medium onion, chopped
2 garlic cloves, crushed
2 eggs
1 tsp chilli powder
¼ cup fresh parsley,
chopped
50g butter

1 Remove the husks from the corn by pulling away; once you have removed the husks, hold the corn upright with one hand and, using a sharp knife, cut away the kernels. Put the sweetcorn kernels in a bowl and add the chopped onion, parsley, chilli and the crushed garlic. Whisk the eggs and mix in. Add the plain flour and sorghum flour and mix thoroughly.

2 Grease a muffin tin generously with butter and add the sweetcorn batter, making sure not to put in too much. Bake the scones in a preheated oven at gas mark 4 (180°C) for 30 minutes or until golden brown. Serve with a meat stew.

Note: Alternatively, you can shallow fry the sweetcorn batter to make sweetcorn fritters.

Pumpkin Snack

250g fresh yellow pumpkin
Pinch of salt
½ cup milk
70g butter
2 cups flour
1½ tsp baking powder
1 egg
50g sugar

1 Remove the seeds from the pumpkin and into chunks. Put the pumpkin in a pot with enough water to cover and boil for 20 minutes or until the pumpkin is tender. Cut the skin away with a sharp knife. The skin is easy to cut from the pumpkin once it has been cooked. Place the pumpkin in a bowl, then mash and leave to cool. Sieve the flour, baking powder and salt in another bowl and add the sugar. Rub in the butter until the mixture looks like fine breadcrumbs.

2 Add the whisked egg and milk to the pumpkin and mix to a smooth batter, then add this to the flour mixture and mix well until you have a mixture which will drop from the back of a tablespoon. Spoon mixture into a well-greased muffin tin and bake in a preheated oven at gas mark 4 (180°C) for 25-30 minutes, or until golden brown.

Onion Snacks (Zambia)

400g flour
1 tsp salt
1 large onion grated or
chopped very finely
50ml water
50g grated cheese

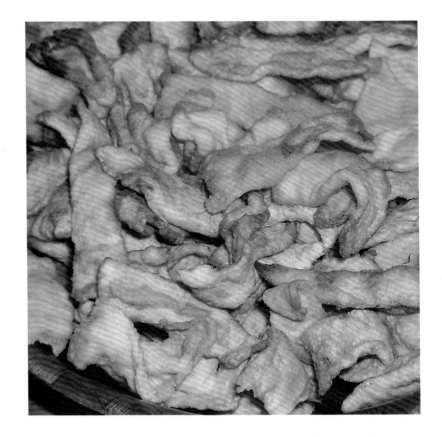

1 Sift flour and salt in the mixing bowl. Add the onion to the flour and mix thoroughly. Make a well in the centre of the dry ingredients and add the water to make a soft, not sticky dough.

2 Roll out the dough thinly and, using a knife, cut into squares. Deep-fry these a little at a time until they are golden brown. Place in saving dish, sprinkle with grated cheese and serve.

Soya Biscuits

75g plain flour
75g soya flour
1 tsp baking powder
6 tbsp caster sugar
4 tbsp butter
1 egg
1 tbsp icing sugar

1 Cream butter and sugar until light and creamy. Gradually add the egg and mix. Sift the two flours with the baking powder, add to the creamy mixture and mix until all the flour is incorporated into the creamy mixture, then knead lightly.

2 Roll out the dough thinly on a floured board using a floured rolling pin and, using a 7.5cm/3inch cutter, cut into round biscuits.

3 Put these on a greased baking tray and bake in the centre of preheated oven at gas mark 4 (180°C) for 30-35 minutes or until golden. Remove from baking tray and cool.

Dust with icing sugar and serve with tea.

Vitumbuwa, African Doughnut (Zambia)

400g plain floor
60g sugar
1 tbsp fast raising yeast
100ml milk
1 egg
Vegetable oil for deep-frying
1 tsp salt

1 Mix the flour, sugar, yeast and salt in a bowl Add the milk to the dry ingredients and mix thoroughly; add the egg to make a butter consistency. Cover the mixture and leave in a warm place overnight.

2 After the mixture has risen, heat the vegetable oil and, using a large spoon, scoop enough mixture and fry until golden brown, remove and place on a large plate. Do this until all the mixture is made into vitumbuwa.

Dust with icing sugar and serve with either a hot or cold drink.

Maize Meal Fruit Cake

75g maize meal flour
1 cup grated coconut
150g plain flour
100g dark brown sugar
250g margarine or butter
125g mixed dried currents
3 eggs
200ml water
1 tsp cinnamon
1 tsp ginger
1 tsp mixed spice
2 tsp baking soda
50ml milk

This is a cake made with maize meal and coconut that can be served as a desert or with afternoon tea.

1 In a heavy saucepan heat 100ml water, add the butter, sugar and the mixed dried fruit, bring to the boil and cook for 15 minutes or until the fruits are plump.

2 In another bowl put the maize meal, add the other 100ml water and make a paste. Add this to the saucepan of hot boiling mixed fruit and mix well. Remove from heat and set aside to cool.

3 In another bowl sieve the flour, cinnamon, ginger and baking soda. When the fruit mix is cool to the touch add the flour and mix well. Beat the eggs separately and add to the batter slowly until they are incorporated in the batter mixture. Add the grated coconut and milk, mix thoroughly. Put the mixture in a small, well-greased loaf tin and bake in a preheated oven at gas mark 4 (180°C) for about 35-45 minutes.

Corn Cake

200g coarse corn flour
100g self-raising flour
250ml fresh cream
100g sugar
100g butter melted
1 tsp baking powder
1 tsp mixed spice
1 tsp nutmeg
1 tsp ginger
4 eggs
Pinch of salt
Icing sugar for dusting

1 Sift the cornflour, self-raising flour, nutmeg, mixed spices, ginger, salt and baking powder in a bowl. Put the sugar, eggs and cream in another bowl and whisk for about 5 minutes.

2 Add the flour slowly until all the flour is incorporated. Once all the flour has been incorporated in the cream mixture add the melted butter to the cake mixture and mix well. Put the mixture in a well-greased tin and bake in a preheated oven at gas mark 4 (180°C) for 30-35 minutes or until the cake is golden brown.

Peanuts And Dried Samp (Botswana And Zambia)

2 cups samp
1 cup peanuts, ground
3 tbsp sugar
300ml milk
Water

1 Wash the samp in plenty of water and soak overnight. Drain the samp, then put in a large pot with enough water to cover and simmer until the samp is tender, about 45 minutes. If water evaporates before the samp is tender, add more water and cook until it is tender.

2 Meanwhile ground the peanuts to a powder consistency with a mortar or coffee grinder. The texture of the peanuts does not have to be completely smooth. Add the milk and the ground peanuts to the samp and simmer for a further 30 minutes or until the peanuts are cooked, stirring occasionally to avoid burning and adding more liquid if required. Add sugar and serve either hot or cold.

Note: Samp is maize that has been broken into small pieces. Samp is widely used in most Southern African recipes and can be used in both sweet and savoury dishes.

Manjase's Tamarind Cake

250g plain flour
200g sweet tamarind
100ml hot water
Juice of 1 lemon
100g brown sugar
2 tbsp maple or golden syrup
200g butter
2 eggs
2 tsp baking soda
3 tbsp milk
1 tbsp ground ginger
1 tsp nutmeg
1 tsp cinnamon

1 Put the 100ml hot water into a saucepan, remove the outer shell of the tamarind and add to the water. Stir vigorously with a wooden spoon, then heat on a very low heat for 10 minutes and stir vigorously again. Strain the tamarind mix through a sieve; using a tablespoon to press the tamarind in the sieve to remove the pulp. Do this until you have removed all the pulp, then discard the seeds. Put the tamarind pulp back in the pan and add the butter, syrup and sugar and simmer for a further 5 minutes or until the butter has melted.

2 In another bowl sieve the flour, cinnamon, ginger and baking soda. When the tamarind mixture is cool to the touch, add the flour and mix well. Beat the eggs separately and add to the batter slowly until they are incorporated in the batter mixture. Put the cake mixture into a baking tin and bake in a preheated oven at gas mark 4 (180°C) for 30-40 minutes or until the cake is golden brown and cooked through. Serve with tea.

Zambian Sweet Potatoes Pudding

2 large sweet potatoes
2 tbsp sugar
1½ cups water
50g butter
¼ cup milk
½ cup roasted groundnuts
½ cup fresh cream

1 Peel the sweet potatoes and cut into cubes. Put the sweet potatoes in a pan with the water and sugar and simmer for 25 minutes or until the sweet potatoes become tender. Drain the sweet potatoes and put in a large pan.

2 Mash the sweet potatoes, put in a mixing bowl and add the butter and milk to the mixture. Roast the groundnuts and grind them to powder by using the coffee grinder. Add them to the sweet potatoes and mix. Put the mixture in a well-greased baking dish and bake in a preheated oven at gas mark 4 (180°C) for 25-30 minutes.

Serve as a pudding, with fresh cream or yoghurt

Baked Sweet Potatoes

2 large sweet potatoes
2 tbsp sugar
1½ cups water
75g butter

1 Peel the sweet potatoes and cut into cubes. Put the sweet potatoes in a pan with the water, sugar and boil for 20 minutes.

2 Drain the water then put the sweet potatoes in an oven proof dish with the butter and gently mix until all the sweet potatoes are coated with butter. Bake in a preheated oven at gas mark 4 (180°C) for 25-30 minutes or until the sweet potatoes are golden brown. Serve as a side dish.

Note: You can use honey in place of sugar.

Maize Meal And Coconut Biscuits

150g maize meal
100g plain flour
100g sugar
50g butter
50g grated coconut
2 large eggs
1 tsp baking powder
Pinch salt
1 tsp ground ginger
1 tsp ground nutmeg

1 Cream butter and sugar until creamy, add the eggs and whisk. In another bowl sift the flour, maize meal and the baking powder. Add the flour mixture to the cream mixture and add the grated coconut and mix to make a firm dough.

2 Roll out the dough and cut into any shape. Place on a greased baking tray and bake in a preheated oven at gas mark 4 (180ºC) for 30-35 minutes or until the biscuits are golden brown.

Serve with tea.

Peanut Snack

1 cup peanuts
50g Sugar
400ml water

1 Start the day by soaking the dry groundnuts in hot water for 30 minutes. Drain the water and place the nuts on a baking tray. Bake the peanuts in a preheated oven at gas mark 4 (180°C) for 30-35 minutes. Set the nuts aside to cool. Once cool, rub the nuts between your hands to remove the skins. Once you have removed all the skins, put the peanuts in a bowl and set aside.

2 Put the sugar in a heavy-based saucepan on a very low heat. Melt the sugar until all the granules have melted and the sugar has acquired a liquid consistency. Once the sugar has melted, and turned light brown, add the peeled nuts and mix thoroughly. Remove from the heat and put the peanuts on a well-greased baking tray. Leave to cool and serve as a snack.

Note: *Handle the hot sugar with care as it burns easily*

Cassava Scones

100g sugar
200g butter or margarine
2 eggs
50g oz. plain flour
200g cassava flour
2 tsp baking powder
100ml water

1 Cream margarine and sugar together until light and fluffy. Add the beaten eggs, a little at a time, beating well between each addition, with a wooden spoon. If the mixture starts to curdle, add a little of the flour.

2 Sift the plain flour; cassava flour and baking powder together in another bowl then fold into the creamy mixture a little at a time quickly and lightly. Spoon the mixture into a greased patty tin until almost full. Bake in a preheated oven at gas mark 4 (180°C) for 30-35 minutes or until the scones are golden brown. Remove from baking tin and cool on a wire tray.

Serve scones with tea.

Fried Vinkwala

1 cup vinkwala (mopani worms)
4 tbsp groundnut oil
1 tsp chilli powder
Salt to taste
Hot water

1 Put vinkwala in a bowl and add enough hot water to cover. Soak vinkwala for 1 hour, drain then rinse under cold water. Set aside to dry.

2 Heat the oil in a heavy based pan and add vinkwala, cook on low heat for 25 - 30 minutes stirring from time to time until the vinkwala are crisp and crunchy, season with salt and chilli. Serve with nshima or as a snack

Mponda

1 cup peanuts
2 mponda
Sugar to taste
Water

1 Put the mponda in a pan filled with water and simmer until the mponda is tender. Drain and keep the mponda in a warm place.

2 Roast the peanuts in a preheated oven at gas mark 4 for 25-30 minutes, then pound in a mortar or food processor to get a rough texture. Cut the mponda in half and serve topped with sugar, and a sprinkle of roasted peanuts.

Kidney Bean And Samp

100g Kidney beans
100g samp
2 tbsp butter
Sugar to taste
Water

1 In separate bowls wash the beans and samp thoroughly. Put the bean in one bowl and add enough water to cover, put the samp in another bowl and add enough water to cover. Soak the ingredients over night.

2 Drain the bean and samp and put in separate pans, add enough water to cover. Simmer the ingredients on low heat for 35 -45 minutes or until tender adding more water when needed. Once all the liquid has evaporated mix the two ingredients, add the butter and sugar and mix. Serve hot as a mid day snack or main meal.

Smoked Fish And Cabbage Stew

2 smoked dried fish
5 cabbage leaves
1 medium onion
2 large tomatoes
1 tsp Curry powder
½ red pepper
1 tsp black pepper
75ml groundnut oil
400ml vegetable stock
Hot water
Salt to taste

1 Soak the fish in hot water for 20 minutes, drain and rinse in cold water. Set aside. Wash the cabbage leaves and set aside. Put the tomatoes, onion, and the red pepper in a food processor and blend to a puree, then set aside.

2 Heat the oil in a large heavy based pan, and the add the puree, cook for 5 minutes, then add the fish, curry powder, black pepper and stock. Simmer for 35 – 40 minute or until the fish is tender. Add the cabbage leaves and simmer for a further 15 – 20 minutes or until the cabbage leaves are tender. Serve with nshima

Note: *the fish needs to be very tender before you add the cabbage leaves, if it is not and you have used all the stock you can add some water and cook until the fish become tender.*

Chicken And Kidney Stew (Zambia)

½ a free range chicken chopped into small pieces
200g kidney chopped into small pieces
2 large tomatoes
1 medium onion chopped
75ml groundnut oil
200ml vegetable stock
1 green pepper chopped
1 ½ tsp black pepper
1 tsp parsley
Salt to taste

1 Put the chicken and kidneys in a large heavy based pan and add 100ml stock, cook on very low heat until the meat is tender and the stock has evaporated (about 25 - 30 minutes). Add the chopped onions, green pepper and the oil and fry until the onions become transparent.

2 Add the tomatoes, salt, black pepper, parsley and cook on low heat for 10 minutes or until the tomatoes are tender. Add the rest of the stock and simmer for a further 15 -25 minutes. Serve with boiled rice or nshima.

Fermented Sorghum Drink

200g sorghum flour
900ml water
Sugar to taste

1 Put 600ml of the water in a pot and heat until the water starts to boil. Mix the other 300ml of the water with the 200g of sorghum flour in a bowl, add this mixture to the boiling water stirring continuously until the mixture becomes porridge. Simmer the porridge for 30 minutes.

2 Remove the porridge from the heat and allow to cool. Put the porridge in a container and seal tightly. Leave the porridge in a cool place for two days to ferment. Put the porridge in the fridge to chill, serve cold with sugar.

Note: *You can also serve the sorghum drink immediately after cooling.*

Central Africa

Central Africa has some of the most delicious
cuisines. Ingredients such as okra, green plantain,
cassava leaves, fafumbwa, cocoyam and sweet potato
are used to make what could only be described as
mouth watering dishes.

Lamb, Chicken And Dried Okra Stew (Chad)

450g free range chicken
450g lamb ribs cut in small
pieces
4 large tomatoes
1 large onion, chopped
2 tbsp dried okra, pounded
to a powder
4 carrots
1 tsp cumin
1 tsp curry powder
1 tsp black pepper
3 dried chillies
4 garlic cloves, crushed
6 tbsp vegetable oil
500ml water
1 stock cube
Salt to taste

Okra is very popular in Chad and is used as the base for many of their stews.

1 In a large heavy based pan put the stock cube, water, curry powder, half chopped onion, one teaspoon salt, the chopped chicken, chopped lamb and cook for 45 minutes. Remove the chicken from the broth and keep in a warm place. Leave the lamb in the broth to simmer for a further 20 minutes. Remove the lamb from the stock and put aside. Do not discard the broth, but put aside for further use.

2 Put the carrots with their skins in another pan with enough water to cover, bring to the boil and simmer for 10 minutes. Once the carrots are tender, drain, leave to cool, then peel, cut into cubes and set aside. In another large pan fry the rest of the chopped onion in 6 tablespoons of oil until the onions are golden brown. Add the chicken and the lamb and fry on low heat for 20 minutes. Pound the dried okra and add to the pan, add the crushed garlic, curry powder and cumin and cook for a further 10 minutes. Add the chopped tomatoes and the crushed chillies and simmer on low heat for 10 minutes. Add the leftover liquid and salt, then simmer for 10 minutes. Add the cooked carrots and cook for a further 10 minutes. Serve with boiled rice.

Mashed Green Plantain

2 green plantains
600ml water

Beef Stew

200g minced beef
5 tbsp vegetable oil
3 tbsp palm oil
2 fresh tomatoes
1 large onion
½ hot pepper
1 tbsp tomato paste
1 red bell pepper
1 stock cube
300ml hot water
2 tbsp thyme
Salt to taste

1 Wash the plantain in their skins, cut them in half and put in a large pan filled with water and boil until the plantain is tender and not mushy – about 35 minutes. Remove the plantain from the water, remove from their skins and immediately put in a mortar and pound until the plantain acquires a smooth, elasticised, sticky texture. If you don't have a mortar simply use a food processor. Transfer the plantain to a steaming bowl and steam for a further 20 minutes. Serve warm with beef stew.

2 Start by blending the bell pepper, hot pepper and tomatoes to a puree. Put the vegetable oil in a large pan, add the onions and fry until they are golden brown. Add the palm oil minced beef and fry on low heat for 20 minutes. Add the puree mixture, thyme and salt and mix, then add the hot water and stock cube and simmer until the liquid has reduced (about 30-40 minutes).

Serve with the mashed green plantain

Vegetable Rice Dish

2 large onions

1 green bell pepper

1 large eggplant cut into bite size pieces

2 large potatoes

7 fresh okra cleaned and tailed

½ cup green peas

1 large carrot chopped into small cubes

2 tsp black pepper

2 large fresh tomatoes, chopped

1 hot pepper

1 tsp dried thyme

4 tsp curry powder

175g basmati rice

75ml palm oil

3 tbsp vegetable oil

Vegetable stock

Salt to taste

Water

1 Wash the rice in cold water and soak for 30 minutes. Then wash in plenty of cold water again. Drain and set aside. Cut the potatoes into small cubes and put into a heavy based pan with enough water to cover, add 3 teaspoons curry powder, 1 teaspoon black pepper, salt and simmer for 10 - 15 minutes. Drain and add vegetable oil and mix making sure to coat each potato with oil. Transfer the potatoes to a baking tray and bake in a preheated oven gas mark 4 (180°c) for 10 - 15 minutes or until golden brown. Transfer to another pan. Set aside.

2 Blend the bell pepper, hot pepper, thyme, 1 teaspoon curry powder the onions and tomatoes to a puree. Put the palm oil in a large pan, add the puree and the salt and cook for 10 minutes. Add the eggplant and okra and cook for 5 minutes, then add 200ml stock and simmer for a further 25 - 30 minutes. Remove the okra and the egg plant from the sauce and add to the pan with the potato.

3 Add the carrots to the sauce and cook until the carrots are tender (about 5 – 10 minutes). Add the rice and peas to the sauce and stir. Add a little stock if needed cover and simmer on very low heat, adding more stock when needed. Do not stir. Cook until the rice is ready. The rice should be light and fluffy. Serve warm with the vegetable on top and, fried yellow plantain

Millet Doughnut (Chad)

100g millet flour
200g wheat flour
1 tbsp. fast raising yeast
150ml honey
150ml water
1 tsp salt
25g butter
4 tbsp plain yoghurt
1 egg
Groundnut oil for deep-frying

1 Place the butter in a saucepan and melt on low heat, add the yoghurt and honey and mix. Remove from the heat and set aside. Sieve and mix the two flours, then add the salt, yeast and mix. Add the cooled butter and yoghurt mixture and mix, break the egg in a bowl, whisk and then add to the doughnut mixture and mix to make a smooth batter.

2 Cover the batter and leave in a warm place for 6 hours. When the batter has risen heat the oil in a large deep pan. Use a teaspoon to scoop the batter into the oil and deep fry until golden brown.

Note: These need to be deep-fried on a medium - low heat, so that they can cook through.

Pumpkin With Peanuts (Chad)

1 cup roasted peanuts
2 cups water
½ a large pumpkin,
cleaned and cut into pieces
½ tsp salt
4 tbsp sugar
Fresh cream or yoghurt to
serve

1 Put the pumpkin in a pan filled with water and ½ teaspoon salt and simmer until the pumpkin is tender. Drain and keep the pumpkin in a warm place.

2 Roast the peanuts in a preheated oven at gas mark 4 for 25-30 minutes, then pound in a mortar or food processor to get a rough texture. Serve the pumpkin hot, topped with white or brown sugar, a sprinkle of roasted peanuts and fresh cream or yoghurt.

Beans, Peanut And Maize Mix

(Central & Southern Africa)

½ cup dried kidney beans
½ cup dry peanuts
1 cup dried maize
1 large onion chopped
1 large tomato chopped
2 tbsp palm oil
1 green chilli chopped
2 garlic cloves, crushed
½ green pepper chopped
1 tsp paprika
¼ tsp black pepper
1 tbsp tomato paste
¼ cup chopped parsley
Juice of half a lemon
Salt to taste

1 In separate bowls wash and soak the dried maize, beans and peanuts overnight. Boil the ingredients in separate pans until tender but not mushy.

2 Drained and mix these ingredients together in a bowl. In another large pan, heat the palm oil, add the crushed garlic, chopped onion, green pepper and chilli and fry until the onions are transparent. Add the chopped tomato, paprika and the tomato paste and simmer for 10 minutes. Add the maize, beans and peanuts then add the black pepper, chopped parsley, lemon juice and salt, and stir.

Serve as a main meal or side dish.

A Spinach And Fish Dish (Central African Republic)

1 cup spinach washed and chopped
1 fresh fish (tilapia)
2 fresh tomatoes
1 tbsp palm oil
½ bell pepper
1 green chilli,
1 onion,
2 tbsp peanut butter
3 tbsp groundnut oil
1 cup water
Salt to taste

1 Wash and chop the spinach and set aside. Cut the fish in half, sprinkle with salt and set aside. Heat a heavy based pan, add the groundnut oil and fry the fish, turning over until evenly cooked, about 5 - 10 minutes on each side. Transfer the fish to a plate and set aside. In the same pan add the chopped onions and fry until they are transparent. Blend the tomato, bell pepper and hot pepper and add to the pan, add the palm oil and simmer for 5 minutes.

2 Add the spinach and cook for a further 5 - 10 minutes. Mix the peanut butter with water and add to the spinach, then add salt. Add the fish and simmer for a further 20 - 25 minutes, stirring occasionally to avoid burning.

Serve with boiled rice or Gari.

Pondu, A Cassava Leaf Dish (Congo)

5 garden eggs, washed thoroughly
1½ cups processed cassava leaves
1 garlic clove crushed
2 smoked dried fish
½ of a whole chicken
¼ cup palm oil
3 spring onions
1 vegetable stock cube
1 green pepper
2 large tomatoes
½ hot pepper, chopped
Salt to taste
Vegetable oil for deep frying
Water

1 Start by soaking the fish in hot water for one hour, then drain, flake fish and set aside. Put the cassava in a pan. Add enough water to cover, bring to the boil and simmer for 1½-2 hours or until the cassava is tender, adding more water when needed.

2 Once the cassava is tender add palm oil, the onion, crushed garlic, the tomatoes and simmer for another 10 minutes. Then add the fish, hot pepper and washed garden eggs. Cook for a further 30 minutes. Chop the chicken into pieces, add 1 teaspoon salt and deep fry until golden brown. Drain on kitchen paper then add the chicken pieces to the cassava and simmer for further 15- 20 minutes. Serve with nshima or pounded yam.

Note: *Spinach can be used in place of cassava leaves, but if using spinach remember it cooks faster than cassava and will therefore require less cooking time.*

Fafumbwa (Congo) Green Vegetables In Peanut Butter

2 cups chopped fafumbwa
(dried green vegetables
found
in the Congo and East
Africa)
3 tbsp peanut paste or
smooth peanut paste
2 tbsp palm oil
Salt to taste
1 vegetable stock cube
3 spring onions
2 tbsp tomato paste
400ml water

1 Soak the vegetables in hot water and wash several times. Put the vegetables in a large pan, add 200ml water and the stock cube and simmer for 30 minutes. Add chopped spring onions, tomato paste and palm oil and simmer for a further 20 minutes.

2 Add the rest of the water and the 3 tablespoons peanut butter on top of the vegetables. Do not stir at this point. Cover and simmer for 10 minutes, and then stir the peanut butter into the vegetables, add salt and cook for a further 20 minutes, stirring from time to time to avoid burning. Serve this dish with cassava stiff porridge.

Note: Collard green or spinach can also be used in place of fafumbwa, but if using spinach remember it cooks faster and will therefore require less cooking time.

Cassava Stiff Porridge

400g maize flour
400g cassava flour
900ml water

1 Put 600ml of the water in a pan and bring to the boil. Mix the other 300ml of the water with the 200g of maize meal in a bowl. Add this mixture to the boiling water, stirring continuously until the mixture becomes porridge.

2 Simmer the porridge for 20 minutes, then mix the rest of maize meal with the cassava and add to the porridge, stirring continuously until it becomes a stiff porridge.

Serve with a meat or vegetable dish.

Rice With Peanuts And Coconut

175g long grain rice
¼ cup peanuts
100ml coconut milk
2 tbsp grated coconut
1 red fresh chilli
6 tbsp vegetable oil
1 onion, chopped
1 tsp salt
Water

1 Put the 2 tbsp vegetable oil and the peanuts in a large pan and fry for 10 minutes, turning from time to time so that they are evenly done. Set aside to cool; when cool rub off and discard the skins. Roast the grated coconut in deep pan until it is golden brown, and set aside.

2 Meanwhile wash the rice in plenty of cold water. Drain and soak rice in boiled hot water for 10 minutes, then drain and rinse the rice again. Fill a pan with water and bring to the boil, add the rice and boil for 3 minutes. Drain and rinse the rice in cold water, then set aside.

3 In another pan heat the rest the vegetable oil. Add the onion and crushed garlic and cook until the onions are transparent. Add the rice and stir, then add the chilli and coconut milk. Cook for 5 minutes, then add 6 tablespoons water, stir and simmer until all the water has been absorbed. Put the rice in a baking dish, add the peanuts and the grated roasted coconut and mix, bake in a preheated oven at gas mark 4 for 25-30 minutes.

Serve with a chicken stew.

Dried Fish In Peanut Stew (Cameroon)

1½ cups small fish or dried sardines
1 red chilli
1 small tomato, chopped
2 tbsp tomato paste
1 onion, chopped
3 tbsp peanut paste or peanut butter
1½ tbsp palm oil
2 tbsp fresh coriander, chopped
2 garlic cloves, crushed
200ml water
Salt to taste

1 Wash and soak the fish in hot water for 30 minutes. Drain, then put the fish with 100ml water in a large, heavy based pan. Simmer for 20 minutes or until all the water has evaporated. Add the palm oil, chopped onions and garlic and fry for 5 minutes, then add the chopped tomatoes, tomato paste, chilli and the rest of the water and simmer for 10 minutes.

2 Add the peanut paste. Do not stir, cover and simmer on very low heat for 20 minutes, then stir the stew and cook for a further 10 minutes, stirring from time to time to avoid burning and adding more water if the stew is too thick. Finish by adding salt and the chopped coriander.

Serve hot with gari or pounded yam

Fried Plantain Parties

2 green plantains
2 cups chicken breast
1 large onion, grated
1 tsp chilli powder
½ bell pepper grated
1 tsp cumin
¼ cup fresh coriander
2 garlic cloves, crushed
1 tsp salt
Groundnut oil for deep frying

1 Mince the chicken and put in a mixing bowl. Pound or process the plantain and add to chicken mince. Add the grated onion and bell and mix.

2 Add the cumin, chopped coriander, crushed garlic and salt to taste and mix. Shape the mixture into small round balls using your hands. Heat the oil in large, heavy pan and, deep fry until they are golden brown. Serve as a side dish or as a snack.

Note: *You can also use a tablespoon, to scoop the mixture into the oil and deep fry until golden brown.*

Mashed Coco Yam And Fried Tilapia

Coco Yam
2 fresh coco yam
600ml water
1 tsp salt

Tilapia
1 large tilapia
¼ cup vegetable oil
1 tsp black pepper
1 medium onion chopped
1 spring onion chopped
2 large tomatoes chopped
Salt to taste
½ hot pepper
1 stock cube
¼ cup water

1 Peel and wash the cocoyam in plenty of water. Cut in quarters and put into a large pan. Add salt and enough water to cover. Bring to the boil and simmer for 25 minutes or until the cocoyam is tender. Mash the cocoyam roughly with a masher and then keep in a warm place.

2 Wash the tilapia, then dust with salt and pepper. Shallow fry the fish until it is golden brown on both sides. Set aside. In the same pan add chopped onion, and fry until onions are transparent, add the chopped tomatoes and hot pepper and cook on a low heat until the tomatoes are tender. Add the stock cube and water and simmer for 5 minutes, then add the fried fish, cover and cook for a further 5 minutes.

Serve the tilapia on a large plate with the sauce and the mashed coco yam.

Coco Yam Crisp And Beef Stew

Coco Yam
2 fresh small cocoyam
600ml water
1 tsp salt
Vegetable oil for deep-
frying

Beef Stew
500g beef
2 medium onions
1 green pepper
1 tbsp curry powder
1 tbsp thyme
1 stock cube
2 large fresh tomatoes
1 small red chilli
3 tbsp palm oil
2 tbsp vegetable oil
2 cups water
Salt to taste

1 Dissolve the salt in the water, and then cut the cocoyam into thin round disks. Put these in the salty water and leave for 1 hour. Drain the cocoyam, then pat dry and deep fry until the cocoyam is crisp and golden brown.

2 Blend the tomatoes, green peppers, the onion and the chilli to make a puree. In a large pan heat the palm oil and the vegetable oil, then add the puree and cook on low heat for 10 minutes. Wash and cut the beef into bite-size pieces, add to the cooking sauce along with the 2 cups water, curry powder, thyme, the stock cube, salt to taste and half of the hot pepper, then simmer on very low heat for 30-40 minutes or until the meat is tender.

Serve with the cocoyam crisp.

Fresh Tilapia Fish With Green Plantain Chips (Congo)

Tilapia
1 large tilapia
1 lemon
¼ cup vegetable oil
25g butter
1 tsp black pepper
1 large onion
1 large tomato
2 garlic cloves, crushed
Salt to taste
½ hot pepper

Plantain Chips
2 green plantains
Salt to taste
Vegetable oil for deep-frying

1 Wash the tilapia, then dust with salt and pepper. Shallow fry the fish until it is golden brown on both sides. Set aside. In the same pan add the butter, and the chopped onion and garlic and fry until onions are transparent. Add the chopped tomatoes and hot pepper and simmer until the tomatoes are cooked. Set aside.

2 Clean the plantain with running water. Peel and chop the plantain into thick disks and deep-fry in vegetable oil until golden brown. Sprinkle with enough salt to taste. Serve the tilapia on a large plate with the sauce poured over, a slice of lemon and the plantain chips.

Roasted Cassava

1 large fresh cassava root
400ml water
1 tsp coarse black pepper
1 tsp chilli powder
(optional)
Salt to taste

1 Peel the cassava, cut in half and put in a large pan filled with water and one teaspoon salt, bring to the boil and simmer for 20 minutes or until the cassava is tender.

2 Remove the cassava from the water and cut roughly, put the cassava on a greased oven tray and roast in a preheated oven at gas mark 5 for 20-25 minutes or until golden brown. Sprinkle with the black pepper and chilli powder and serve as a snack.

Note: Cassava skin can be tough, so use a small sharp knife to peel slowly and carefully and wash after you peel. It may also be very difficult to cut the cassava into small pieces before it is cooked, so boil first.

Chicken And Sweet Potato Stew

600g chicken
½ large onion, chopped
2 garlic clove, crushed
2 large fresh tomatoes
1 large sweet potato
1 cup water
3 tbsp peanut paste or peanut butter
3 tbsp palm oil
2 tbsp vegetable oil for frying
1 fresh green chilli
Salt to taste

1 Chop the chicken into bite-size pieces and put in a bowl. Then put 2 tablespoons vegetable oil in a large heavy-based pan and fry the chicken until it is golden brown. Remove the chicken from the pan and keep in a warm place. Add the palm oil to the same pan, then add the onion and garlic and cook until the onions are light brown. Add the tomatoes, salt and chilli and simmer for 5 minutes.

2 Clean the sweet potato and chop into cubes. Add to the sauce, then add the fried chicken and stir. Add water and simmer for 5 minutes, then add the peanut paste and simmer for another 5 minutes. Do not stir. After 5 minutes stir the stew, then simmer for a further 20-30 minutes, stirring from time to time to avoid burning. If the sauce is too thick, add some more water. When the stew is ready the sweet potatoes should be tender and not mushy. Serve stew with boiled rice.

Tip: *Peanut paste or peanut butter burns easily, so do not stir once you add to sauce. Simmer first for about 10 minutes, then stir occasionally while you simmer. If the sauce becomes too thick, add more water to thin.*

Oxtail Stew

500g oxtail cut into pieces
1 stock cube
1 tsp black pepper
2 large fresh tomatoes
2 medium onions
75ml groundnut oil
400ml vegetable stock
Salt to taste

1 Clean the oxtail and cut into pieces. Put in a large heavy based pan and add 200ml stock and black pepper. Cook on a very low heat until the meat becomes tender and all the water has evaporated (about 30- 35 minutes).

2 Add the chopped onions and the oil and fry until the onions turn light brown. Add the tomatoes and cook on low heat for 5- 10 minutes or until tomatoes are tender. Add the rest of the stock and simmer for a further 15 -25 minutes.

Sweet Potato Leaves

2 cup fresh sweet potato leaves
1 fresh green chilli
1 small onion
1 large tomato
6 tbsp groundnut oil
100ml water
Salt to taste

1 Wash the sweet potato leaves and set aside to dry. Heat the oil in a heavy based pan and add the sweet potato leaves, fry for 5 minute stirring to avoid burning. Blend the onion, tomato and chilli to a puree and add to the sweet potato leaves, cook for 5 minutes stirring all the time.

2 Add the water, cover and simmer for 20 – 25 minutes stirring from time to time, season with salt.

Serve with the oxtail and gari or nshima.

Western Africa

West African cuisine is rich with traditional African ingredients. Ingredients such as plantain, egusi seeds, yam, palm oil, bitter leaf, and crawfish are used to make rich stews and soups.

Yam Pottage (Nigeria)

800g. Fresh yam
2 small Potatoes
2 yellow plantain peeled
and cut into thick disks
400ml water
1 tsp salt
1 tsp palm oil

1 Start by peeling the yam and the potatoes and cutting into cubes. Put the water in a large pan and add the salt. Put the potatoes at the bottom of the pan, then the yam on top of the potatoes and the plantain on top of the yam. Simmer for 25-30 minutes or until all the ingredients are tender but not mushy.

2 Once they are tender, add the palm oil , then use a wooden spoon, to stir vigorously until all the ingredients are mixed together.

Serve as a main meal with a meat or vegetable stew.

Spinach And Minced Beef (Nigeria)

4 cups small leaf spinach
2 large tomatoes
1 tsp curry powder
200g minced beef
1 large onion
1 small smoked dried fish
½ cup fresh crawfish, shelled
1 tsp dried crawfish
1 stock cube
1 tsp ground hot pepper
5 tbsp palm oil
Salt to taste

1 Blend the onion, tomato and hot pepper to a puree, then heat the palm oil in a large heavy based pan and add the pureed ingredients and the curry powder. Cook on a low heat for 10 minutes. Add the minced beef, stir and cook for 20 minutes. Meanwhile chop the spinach and wash in plenty of water to remove all sand, then soak in hot water for 10 minutes. Drain and squeeze the spinach to remove excess water and set aside. Clean the smoked fish, remove the head and soak in hot water for 20 minutes, drain, then flake and set aside.

2 Add the fresh crawfish, dried crawfish, the flaked smoked fish and stock cube to the beef and cook for a further 10 minutes, then add the spinach and mix well. Simmer for a further 5 - 10 minutes, then serve with the pounded porridge or gari.

Note: Tiger prawns were used to garnish this recipe, but you can add to the stew for a richer dish.

A Goat Meat And Vegetable Stew (Nigeria)

500g goat meat
2 large tomatoes
1 small hot pepper
2 large onions, chopped
1 green pepper
75ml palm oil
2 cups hot water
1 tsp black pepper
2 tsp dried thyme
2 tsp curry powder
4 cups fresh spinach
200ml vegetable stock
Salt to taste

1 Put the hot pepper, tomatoes, one onion, and the green pepper in a food processor and process until the vegetables are pureed, set aside. In a large pan put the vegetable stock, thyme, half the hot pepper, half the onion, curry powder, black pepper and the goat meat. Cook on a low heat until the goat meat becomes tender (about 45 minutes), then remove the meat from the stock. Do not throw away the stock but set it aside for later use.

2 Heat the palm oil in a large, cast-iron pan, and fry the goat meat for 5 minutes over a low heat. Add the reminder of the onion and continue to fry until the onion is light brown. Add the puree and cook on medium heat for 10 minutes, stirring occasionally to avoid burning. Add the reserved stock and simmer for a further 25-30 minutes Meanwhile, soak the spinach in hot water for 5 minutes, then rinse thoroughly, separate, rinse again (and even a third time if you want to be extra careful), and shred coarsely. Add the spinach to the pan and simmer over medium heat for a further 10 -15 minutes.

Serve with pounded yam or gari.

Goat Meat Soup (Nigeria)

500g goat meat
1 tsp curry powder
1 tsp thyme
1 stock cube
2 large fresh tomatoes
½ a hot pepper
2 medium onions
1 green pepper
75ml palm oil
5 tbsp vegetable oil
400ml water
Salt to taste

1 Blend the tomatoes, green peppers, half the onion, and half the hot pepper to a puree. In a large pan put 400ml water, the goat meat, curry powder, thyme, the stock cube and the half the hot pepper. Simmer for 30-45 minutes or until the meat is tender. Remove the meat from the liquid and set aside. Do not throw away liquid, leave this in the pan for later use.

2 In another large pan fry the chopped onion in 5 tablespoons vegetable oil until the onions are golden brown. Add the palm oil and the goat meat and fry on a low heat for 10 minutes. Add the pureed ingredients, salt and the leftover broth from the goat meat and simmer until the liquid is reduced about 30 minutes.

Serve with gari or pounded yam.

Egusi Soup (Nigeria)

½ cup fresh prawns
500g chicken or a whole
medium sized chicken
½ cup chopped lamb
1 dried smoked fish
1 cup fresh spinach
½ cup fresh prawns
75ml palm oil
2 tbsp vegetable oil
1 stock cube
300ml water
2 tsp curry powder
½ cup ground egusi
2 tsp thyme
½ hot pepper
1½ large onions
2 large fresh tomatoes
Salt to taste

1 In a large, heavy based pan put the stock cube, the water, 1 tsp curry powder, half a chopped onion, salt, the chopped chicken and the lamb and cook for 5 minutes. Remove the chicken from the liquid and set aside. Leave the lamb to boil for a further 20 minutes or until it is tender. Meanwhile soak the smoked dried fish and spinach in two separate bowls in hot water for 10 minutes. Remove and wash the fish in running water. Flake the dried fish with your hands and set aside. Drain and squeezes spinach to remove excess water and set aside. After 20 minutes remove the lamb from pan and set aside.

2 In a large frying pan fry half the chopped onion, the chicken and the lamb in vegetable oil until golden brown, add the palm oil, 1 tsp curry powder and thyme, and cook for a further 5 minutes. Blend the tomatoes, the remaining half of onion and the hot pepper to a puree and add to the meat. Add the flaked dried fish, prawns and spinach and cook for 10 minutes. Add the leftover liquid, ground egusi and salt then simmer for 5 minutes.

Serve hot with pounded yam.

Bitter Leaf And Egusi Soup (Nigeria)

500g goat meat
1 dried smoked fish
1 tbsp dried crawfish
½ fresh crawfish
½ cup egusi (melon seeds)
5 tbsp palm oil
1 onion, chopped
½ hot pepper
1 stock cube
Salt to taste
2 tbsp bitter leaf
300ml water

1 In a large pan put the water, goat meat, half the chopped onion, half the hot pepper and the stock cube and boil until the goat meat is tender (about 45 minutes). Set aside. In another pan heat the palm oil and add the remainder of the onion, the egusi and crushed dried crawfish and cook for 20 minutes.

2 Soak the smoked fish in very hot water for 20 minutes. Drain and wash the fish thoroughly and flake with your hands. Add the egusi mixture to the goat meat and cook for a further 20 minutes. Add the fresh crawfish, smoked fish and salt and mix thoroughly. Add the bitter leaf and simmer for a further 20 minutes.

Serve with pounded yam.

Fish With Hot Peppers (Nigeria)

200g Fish fillets
¼ cup fresh thyme chopped
½ red bell pepper
1 hot pepper
2 tbsp tomato Paste
2 fresh tomatoes chopped
3 medium onions
150ml vegetable stock
4 tbsp palm oil
Salt to taste

1 Season the fish with the salt and the thyme and set aside. Heat the oil in a large pan and add the chopped bell peppers, hot pepper, tomatoes, tomato paste and onion and cook for 10 minutes over moderate heat.

2 Add the stock and simmer on low heat for 15 more minutes. Add the fish slices and simmer for a further 10 minutes. Add salt to taste and serve.

Best Served with boiled rice and a salad.

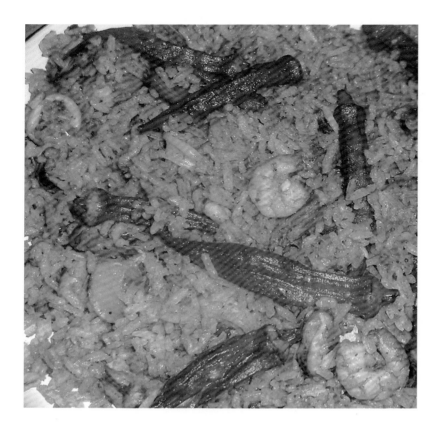

A Rice And Fish Dish (West Africa)

400g long grain rice
½ cup crabmeat
1 cup prawns
100g salt fish
½ cup fresh shrimp
1 heaped tbsp palm oil
3 tbsp vegetable oil
½ hot pepper
1 large onion
½ bell pepper
2 tsp curry powder
1 tsp salt
1 tsp turmeric
12 okra (lady fingers)
½ cup chopped fresh coriander
1 tbsp tomato paste
1 cup vegetable stock

1 Soak the salt fish over night, changing the water at least five times to remove the salt from the fish. After you have removed most of the salt from the fish put it in a large pan filled with boiling water and leave the fish to soak for 30 minutes. Wash and soak the fresh okra in very hot water for 20 minutes. Meanwhile wash the rice in plenty of cold water. Soak rice in boiled hot water for 10 minutes, drain and rinse the rice again. Fill a pan with water and bring to the boil, add the rice and boil for 3 minutes. Remove the rice and rinse in cold water, drain then set aside.

2 Put the chopped hot peppers, bell pepper, onions and coriander in a mortar and pound to a pulp or, if you do not have a mortar, blend the ingredients to a puree. Put the palm oil and vegetable oil in a large pan and add the blended ingredients, curry and tomato paste and simmer for 10 minutes. Add the okra and the salt fish, cook for 10 minutes, then add the crabmeat, shrimp and prawns, and cook for a further 10 minutes. Reduce the heat, add the rice to the pan, stir in the stock and simmer on very low heat, stirring the rice sparingly, as needed, to avoid burning. When rice is ready, serve hot with fried yellow plantain.

Spiced Chicken Stew (Gambia)

300g chicken breast, chopped
1 large onion, chopped
2 medium tomatoes, chopped
1 tsp ground black pepper
1 fresh red chilli
4 tbsp vegetable oil
2 tbsp palm oil
3 tbsp peanut butter
1 tbsp sugar
2 tbsp tomato past
1 cup water
Salt to taste

1 Heat the vegetable oil in a large, heavy based pan and add the chopped chicken. Fry on very low heat until the chicken is evenly browned. Add the palm oil and chopped onion and continue frying until the onions become soft. Then add the chopped tomatoes and simmer for 8 minutes.

2 Add ½ cup water, tomato paste, sugar, chopped chilli, black pepper and salt, then simmer for a further 5 minutes. Mix the other ½ cup water with the peanut butter and add to the chicken. Simmer for 15 minutes, stirring from time to time to avoid burning and adding more water if the stew is too thick.

Serve with boiled rice.

A Peanut, Chicken And Rice Dish (Ghana)

200g chicken
200g basmati rice
3 tbsp palm oil
1 tbsp crunchy peanut butter
2 tbsp tomato paste
1 large onion
4 cloves garlic, crushed
1 tsp cumin powder
1 tsp curry powder
1 tsp coriander powder
1 tsp black pepper
1 stock cube
400ml water
1 fresh red chilli
Salt to taste

1 Cut the chicken into small pieces and set aside. Put half the chopped onion, cumin, coriander, chilli, stock cube, curry, black pepper and chicken in a pan with 400ml water and simmer on low heat for 20 minutes. Meanwhile soak the rice in hot water for 30 minutes, rinse in plenty of cold water, drain and set aside.

2 Remove the chicken from the broth. Reserve the broth for later use in the dish. Transfer the chicken to another pan and add 3 tablespoons palm oil, crushed garlic, and chopped onion and fry ingredients on low heat for 10 minutes. Add the rice to the pan with the chicken and stir, add the tomato paste, peanut butter, salt, the broth and water if needed and stir. Cover and simmer on low heat until all the liquid has evaporated. Check if rice is cooked by testing if it is tender. If so, it is cooked, if not then add a little more water as needed and simmer until all the liquid has evaporated and rice is tender.

Salt Fish And Spinach (Nigeria)

200g dried salt fish
1 large tomato
1 large onion chopped
½ hot pepper
½ green pepper
4 tbsp palm oil
4 tbsp vegetable oil
1 tsp coriander
1 tsp cumin
1 cup fresh spinach,
100 ml vegetable stock
1 tsp curry powder
Salt if needed

1 Soak the fish in water and leave overnight. Change the water 3 to 4 times to remove the excess salt. Blend the tomatoes, half the onion, and peppers to a puree

2 In a large heavy based pan heat the palm oil and vegetable oil and fry the other half of the onion until golden brown. Add the puree, curry powder, cumin and coriander and simmer for 10 minutes. Meanwhile wash and soak the spinach in hot water for 10 minutes. Remove the spinach from the water, making sure to squeeze out excess water, cut coarsely and set aside. Remove the fish from the water and give one final rinse. Cut the fish into chunks and add to the cooking sauce. Add the stock, then simmer for 30 minutes. Add the spinach and cook for a further 15 minutes. Serve with gari or pounded yam.

Note: Salt fish contains a lot of salt, so taste first to see if any more is needed.

Sweet Potato And Seafood Dish (Sierra Leone)

2 large sweet potatoes
3 green bananas
1 cup fresh spinach
200g fresh prawns
100g fresh crawfish
2 fresh red chillies
3 garlic cloves
Vegetable oil for deep-frying
3 tbsp palm oil
1 large onion
100ml vegetable broth
1 cup parsley
Salt to taste

1 Wash the sweet potatoes and cut into thick round disks. Sprinkle with salt and deep fry until they are golden brown. Put on a large plate. Peel the banana, with a small knife, cut into thin disks and deep fry until golden brown, then add to the plate with the sweet potato, keep in a warm place.

2 Heat the palm oil in a large saucepan, add the chopped onion and garlic, then fry until the onion is transparent. Blend the tomatoes and chilli, add to the pan and cook on low heat 20 minutes. Wash the spinach thoroughly and soak in hot water for 5 minutes. Drain and add the chopped spinach to the sauce and cook for 10 minutes. Add the prawns, crawfish and salt, then simmer for a further 10 minutes. Add the parsley and stir thoroughly. Serve the sweet potatoes, bananas and seafood on a large plate as a main meal.

Steam Tilapia Fillet With Yellow Plantain Chips

Yellow Plantain Chips

2 yellow plantain
1 tsp hot pepper
Salt to taste
Oil for frying

Steam Tilapia Fillet

1 fresh tilapia
3 medium tomatoes
1 medium onion
1 tsp coarse black pepper
Salt to taste
¼ tsp hot pepper or chilli powder
Vegetable oil
2 tbsp Palm oil
3 eggs

1 Peel plantain and rub with salt and hot pepper. Chop the plantain into thick disks and deep-fry until golden brown, then drain on grease proof paper. Keep the plantain in a warm place as you prepare the rest of the dish.

2 Clean the tilapia and cut off the head. Remove the flesh by using a large, sharp knife, holding down the tail and cutting the flesh from the tail. Keeping close to the fish bone, cut off as much flesh as possible from both sides of the fish. Once you have removed the flesh, put the fish bone and head in a plastic bag. You can now keep it in the freezer for stock. Put the tilapia fillets in a bowl and add salt and black pepper. Put the fillets in a steamer and steam for 20 minutes.

3 Break the eggs into a bowl, add salt to taste, whisk the eggs briefly then fry until they are firm. Set aside. Blend the onion, hot pepper and the tomatoes to a puree. Heat the palm oil in a saucepan and add the puree. Simmer on very low heat for 20 minutes, add salt and serve on a large plate with the fried plantain, egg, and fish.

Eba (Gari)

800g Gari
900ml water

1 Heat the water in a pan and let it come to the boil. Remove the pan from the heat and add the gari. Mix well, stand for 5 minutes, then stir vigorously to make a stiff porridge. Serve with any stew in this book.

Note: If the stiff porridge is too soft then add more gari, if it is too hard add some more boiling water to get a dough like consistency.

Inyan (Pounded Yam)

800g pounded yam flour
900ml water

1 Heat the water in a pot and let it come to the boil. Add the yam flour and stir vigorously until you have a stiff porridge. Serve with any stew in the book.

Note: you will need a special wooden spoon used to cook African stiff porridge to get the best results.

Beans Dish

(Nigeria)

150g peeled black eye beans
1 smoked dried fish
300g chicken chopped into bite size pieces
2 fresh tomatoes
1 tsp curry powder
1 large onion chopped
½ hot pepper
200ml vegetable stock
2 tbsp palm oil
4 tbsp vegetable oil
Salt to taste

1 Put the beans in a large pan, add enough water to cover and bring to the boil. Simmer the beans for 1½ hours or until tender, adding more water when needed. In another large pan heat the palm oil, add half the onion and fry for one minute. Blend the tomatoes and the other half of the onion, add to the palm oil and cook for 10 minutes.

2 Add the beans, hot pepper, curry powder, salt, stock and simmer for 25-30 minutes, stir occasionally to avoid burning. Put the beans in a mortar or blender and blend to a fine puree. Set aside. Rub some salt into the chicken and fry in vegetable oil until golden brown, then set aside. Soak the dried fish in very hot water for 30 minutes, drain, flake the fish with your hands and set aside. Add the fried chicken and the fish to the beans and cook for a further 10 - 15 minutes, stirring from time to time to avoid burning. Serve with pounded yam or gari.

For instructions on peeling black eye beans see page 110

Okra With Egusi And Fish

20 fresh okra fingers
¼ cup fresh crawfish, shelled
1 small smoked fish, cleaned and chopped
1 tsp ground egusi seeds
150ml water
Salt

Beef Stew

200g beef chopped into very small pieces
300g chicken breast chopped in piceces
1 tbsp dried ground crawfish
1 small smoked dried fish, soaked flaked
3 tbsp palm oil
6 tbsp vegetable oil
1 large onion chopped
½ bell pepper
½ hot pepper
300ml vegetable stock
Salt

1 Wash the okra thoroughly, then grate or blend in a food processor until smooth. Heat the water in a pan and add the okra. Cook for 10 minutes, then add the dried smoked fish, crawfish, salt and the egusi seeds and cook for a further 10 minutes.

2 Blend the tomatoes, bell pepper, crawfish, half the onion and half the hot pepper. In a large pan put 300ml stock and boil the beef with the curry powder, thyme and the rest of the hot pepper. Boil until the meat is tender. Remove the meat from the stock and set aside. Put the stock in a jug for later use. In another pan, fry the chicken in the vegetable oil until golden brown then set aside. Put the rest of the onion in the same pan and fry until golden brown; add the beef and fry for about 10 minutes. Add the chicken, the palm oil, the fish, the blended tomato mixture and some of the liquid and simmer for 25-30 minutes.

Serve beef stew with okra and gari, or yam.

Jollof Rice (West Africa)

1.4kg chicken or a medium whole chicken
2 large onions
1 green bell pepper
½ cup fresh shrimps
1 cup fresh prawns
1 carrot, finely chopped
1 tsp black pepper
2 large fresh tomatoes, chopped
1 hot pepper
1tsp dried thyme
1 tsp curry powder
175g basmati rice
75ml palm oil
4 tbsp vegetable oil
300ml vegetable stock
Salt to taste

1 Cut the chicken into quarters and put into a heavy based pan with the vegetable stock, curry powder thyme, one chopped onion and salt and simmer for 20 minutes. Remove the chicken from the stock and fry in vegetable oil until golden brown. Set aside. Do not throw away stock but keep it for use later in the recipe. Blend the bell pepper, the rest of the onion and tomatoes to a puree. Put the palm oil in a large pan, add the puree and cook for 10 minutes. Cut the carrots into very small cubes and add to the cooking sauce, then add the stock and cook until the carrots are tender (about 15 minutes). Add the prawns and shrimps and cook for another 5 minutes.

2 Meanwhile wash the rice in cold water and soak in boiling water for 30 minutes. Then wash in plenty of cold water. Drain and add to the pan with shrimp and prawn and stir. Add a little water if needed and simmer on very low heat, stirring rice sparingly, as needed, to avoid burning. When rice is almost ready put the fried chicken pieces on top of the rice. Do not stir and cook until the rice is ready. The rice should be light and fluffy. Serve hot with fried yellow plantain.

Fresh Tilapia, Sweet Corn And Hot Pepper Sauce (Ghana)

1 large fresh bream fish

1 red pepper

½ hot pepper

3 large tomatoes

1 tbsp ground dried crawfish

250g fresh sweet corn or maize kernels

4 spring onions

100ml water

5 tbsp vegetable oil

3 tbsp palm oil

Salt to taste

1 In a blender, blend the crawfish, red pepper and hot pepper, water, the onion, and the tomatoes to a puree. Heat the palm oil in a saucepan, add the puree and simmer for 20 minutes. Add the sweetcorn kernels and salt and then simmer for a further 15 minutes.

2 Clean the fish, then rub some salt on the skin and fry in vegetable oil until it is golden brown on both sides. Serve hot with sweetcorn and hot pepper sauce.

Akara (Nigeria)

550g black eye beans
1 large onion
½ a hot pepper or chilli
½ fresh green pepper
1 stock cube
100ml water
Salt to taste
Vegetable oil for frying

1 Soak the beans in water for 20 - 30 minutes then transfer the beans to a large bowl filled with water, remove the skins by rubbing the beans in both hands so that the skins can float to the top, discard the skins that float to the top. Repeat this process until you have removed all the skins.

2 Once you have removed all the skins, soak the beans for a further 2 hours, then drain and place the beans in a mortar or blender with 100ml water and blend until the beans look like porridge. Add the hot pepper and vegetable stock cube and blend. Transfer the mixture to a bowl, then add the finely chopped onion, green pepper and salt and mix well. Use a tablespoon to make the akara. Scoop some of the mixture and deep fry in batches in a large pan until akara is golden brown. Akara is best served warm.

In Nigeria akara is served for breakfast with akamu. Akamu is a custard made from maize or corn.

Kidney Beans Akara

2 cups kidney beans
1 small onion finely chopped
½ green pepper
1 stock cube
100ml water
1 small chilli
Groundnut oil for frying
Salt if needed

1 Wash the beans, then put in a bowl with enough water to cover, soak the beans over night. Drain and place the beans in a mortar or blender with 100ml water and blend until the beans look like porridge.

2 Add the stock cube and the green pepper, chilli and blend again. Transfer the mixture to a bowl, then add the finely chopped onion, and salt if needed mix well.

3 Use a tablespoon to scoop some of the mixture and and fry in batches in a large pan until akara is golden brown.

Salad

6 lettuce leaves
1 large tomato finely chopped
1 spring onion finely chopped
Juice of 1 lemon
2 tbsp olive oil
Salt to taste

1 Wash the lettuce leaves and set aside to dry, then transfer to a salad bowl. Add the tomatoes and onions and mix.

2 Mix the lemon juice with the olive oil then pour over the salad and mix thoroughly, add salt to taste and serve with warm akara.

Hot Pepper Flavoured Rice

200g basmati rice
1 tbsp tomato paste
1 onion, chopped
1 clove garlic, chopped
4 tbsp palm oil
1 tsp curry powder
¼ cup fresh coriander
½ hot pepper
1 red pepper
1 stock cube
200ml chicken stock
Water

1 Soak the rice in hot water for 20 minutes, rinse and soak again in hot water for another 10 minutes, then rinse in plenty of water.

2 Put the palm oil in a pan, add the onion and fry until the onion becomes light brown. Add the finely chopped red pepper, hot pepper, crushed garlic, curry powder, chopped fresh coriander and stir for one minute. Add the rinsed and drained rice to the pan, the tomato paste, salt and the stock and stir. Bring to the boil, then simmer on low heat until all the liquid has been absorbed. The rice should be fluffy; if not add a little more water and simmer. Serve with any soup or stew.

Garden Egg And Potatoes Stew

6 garden eggs
1 large onion, chopped finely
2 large tomatoes
1 green bell pepper
5 tbsp palm oil
1 tsp curry powder
1 fresh red chilli
2 large potatoes
1 cup fresh, small leaf spinach
1 stock cube
300ml water

1 Put the palm oil in a large heavy-based pan, add the onion and cook for 5 minutes. Blend the fresh tomatoes, bell pepper and chilli to a puree then add the puree to the pan and simmer on low heat for 10 minutes.

2 Meanwhile prepare the garden eggs by washing them thoroughly to remove any earth, then put them in a large pan filled with water and boil them for 20 minutes. After 20 minutes drain the garden eggs and put them in cold water to cool. Once they are cool peel the skins off with a small knife and remove the stems, then set aside. Soak the spinach in hot water for 10 minutes, then drain and set aside. Wash and peel the potatoes, then cut into cubes and add to the cooking tomato sauce. Add the curry powder, the stock cube, salt and 300ml water and cook for 20 minutes. Add the garden eggs and spinach and stir for 5 minutes, then simmer for a further 20 minutes or until the potatoes are tender.

Serve as a main dish, starter or side dish.

Moi Moi, Steamed Black Eye Bean (Nigeria)

550g dried black eye beans
1 medium onion
½ fresh hot pepper or 1 small red chilli
¼ cup kidney, fried and chopped into small pieces
½ cup chicken, fried and chopped into small pieces
1 small smoked dried fish
1 stock cube
1 tsp dried crawfish, ground
½ cup fresh crawfish shelled
2 tbsp palm oil
Salt to taste
1 tsp hot pepper powder
150ml water
3 boiled eggs, chopped

1 Soak the beans in water for 20 - 30 minutes then transfer the beans to a large bowl filled with water, remove the skins by rubbing the beans in both hands so that the skins can float to the top, discard the skins that float to the top. Repeat this process until you have removed all the skins. Soak the beans for a further 8 hours or overnight, then drain and put the beans in a mortar or blender with the 150ml water and blend to a smooth, almost grainy consistency. Add the hot peppers and continue to blend. Meanwhile soak the dried fish in hot water for 30 minutes, drain and wash in cold water, then flake fish with your hands and set aside.

2 Heat the palm oil in a saucepan for 2 minutes and add to the bean mixture. Add the chopped onions, salt and pepper. Add the fried chicken, the liver, the fresh crawfish, the flaked fish, crawfish, the boiled egg and mix thoroughly. Scoop about 2-3 tablespoons of the mixture onto a banana leaf or foil or into small plastic bags. Wrap securely with string and steam for one hour.

Serve as a starter or a side dish.

Pepper Soup (West Africa)

500g free range chicken breast, chopped into very small pieces
200g beef, chopped into very small pieces
1 tsp curry powder
1 tsp thyme
1 stock cube
2 large fresh tomatoes
1 hot pepper
1 large onion
1 green pepper
4 tbsp palm oil
600ml water
Salt to taste

1 Blend the tomatoes, green peppers, half the onion and the hot pepper to a puree. Put the palm oil in a large pan, add the other half onion and fry until transparent. Add the blended puree and cook for 10 minutes.

2 Add the chopped chicken, beef, curry powder, thyme and salt and simmer for 10 minutes. Then add the stock cube and water and simmer on very low heat for 1½ hours.

Serve with yam porridge.

Chin Chin
(Nigeria)

4 cups plain flour
1 cup sugar
1 cup evaporated milk
1 egg
25g butter
Pinch of salt
Groundnut oil for deep
frying

1 Mix the flour, butter and pinch of salt in a bowl and rub in until the mixture resembles bread crumbs. Then add the sugar and mix thoroughly. In another bowl whisk the milk and egg.

2 Add the milk and egg mixture a little at a time to the flour mixture until you have a non-sticky dough. Leave the dough to rest for 30 minutes, then roll out thinly on a floured board. Cut the dough into small squares and deep fry a few at a time until golden brown, do this until all the dough is made into chin chin. Put in a serving dish and serve with a cold drink.

Note: You can use milk in place of the evaporated milk.

Gari Drink

6 tbsp gari
1 tbsp sugar
½ cup cold milk
½ cup cold water

1 In a large cup put the gari, sugar, milk and water and mix well. Serve immediately with lots of ice on a sunny day.

Chicken Gizzard Stew

200g chicken gizzards
200g chicken livers
1 small hot pepper
1 tsp black pepper
2 tsp dried thyme
100ml vegetable stock
1 onion
2 large tomatoes
75ml groundnut oil
1 tsp black pepper
Salt to taste

1 Wash the gizzards and livers thoroughly and set aside. Put the oil in a large heavy based pan and fry the gizzards and giblets for 5 – 10 minutes.

2 Blend the pepper, onion, and tomatoes and add to the pot with the gizzards and giblets. Add black pepper, thyme, stock and salt then simmer for 20 to 25 minutes. Serve with nshima or pounded yam.

Hot Pepper Beef

300g Beef
1 medium onion
2 medium tomatoes
1 tsp black pepper
1 fresh hot pepper
2 tbsp palm oil
1 tbsp curry powder
1 tsp thyme
1 green pepper
2 tsp ground dried crawfish
50 ml vegetable stock
Salt to taste

1 Put the onion, tomatoes, curry powder, thyme, hot pepper, black pepper and green pepper in a blender and blend the ingredients to a puree. Wash the beef and cut into thin strips, then put in a large heavy based pan, add the blended ingredients, palm oil, stock, dried crawfish and salt.

2 Cook the beef until all the liquid has evaporated about 25 – 30 minutes. Transfer the beef to a barbecue or grill and barbecue until the meat is completely dry turning from time to time to avoid burning. Serve as a snack or as a starter.

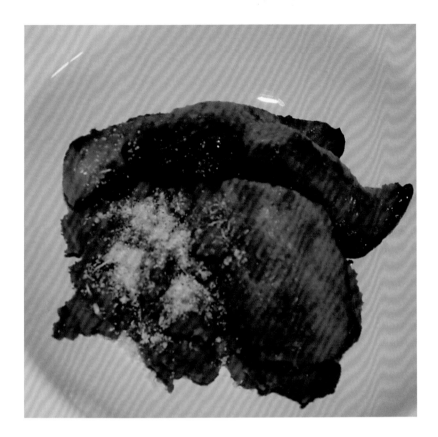

Roasted Plantain, Beans And Gari

2 plantains
2 chicken thighs
2 tbsp gari
2 cup brown beans
2 tbsp vegetable oil
¼ tsp ground hot pepper
1 tbsp palm oil
Salt to taste
Water

1 Wash the bean and put in a large pan, add enough water to cover. Simmer for 30 -35 minutes or until tender, adding more water when needed. Once all the water has evaporated add the palm oil and salt if needed and mix, set aside.

2 Peel the plantain and cut into thick disks, add the vegetable oil, salt and hot pepper and mix. Transfer the plantain to a roasting tin. Roast the plantain in a preheated oven for gas mark 4 (180°c) for 15 – 20 minutes. Put the plantain on a plate with the beans on the side and sprinkle the gari on the beans.

Serve with roasted chicken.

Okra And Kidney Beans

200g kidney beans
1 tsp curry powder
1 tsp chilli powder
3 large tomatoes finely chopped
2 tbsp tomato paste
1 large onion finely chopped
70ml vegetable oil
Salt to taste
Water

1 Wash the beans and soak overnight. Drain the beans and transfer to a large pan, add the oil, tomatoes, onions, curry powder, tomato paste, salt and enough water to cover, simmer for 11/2 - 2 hours or until the beans is very tender.

2 Check the beans from time to time and stir to avoid burning. Add more water if needed. The beans should be tender and the sauce should be thick.

Okra

20 fresh okra fingers
1 large tomato finely chopped
½ a small onion finely chopped
150ml water
Salt to taste

1 Wash the okra thoroughly, then grate or blend in a food processor until smooth. Heat the water in a pan and add the okra, tomatoes and onions.
Cook on low heat for 15 - 20 minutes stirring from time to time to avoid the okra from boiling over. Add the salt and serve.

Serve the okra in a deep plate with the beans on top, this dish is best served with nshima or gari

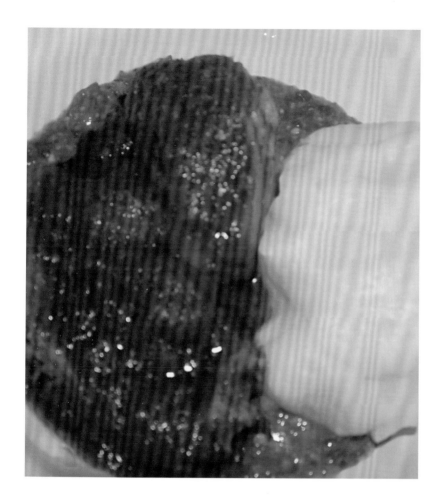

Cow Trotters And Tripe Stew With Okra

500g cow trotters chopped into pieces
200g trip cleaned and cut into medium pieces
(tripe)
2 large tomatoes
1 small hot pepper
2 medium onions, chopped
1 green pepper
2 tbsp palm oil
5 tbsp vegetable oil
1 tsp black pepper
2 tsp dried thyme
2 tsp curry powder
1 tbsp dried craw fish
400ml vegetable stock
Salt to taste

Okra
20 fresh okra fingers, blended or grated
150ml water
Salt to taste

1 Put the hot pepper, craw fish, tomatoes, 1 onion, and the green pepper in a food processor and blend to a puree, set aside. In a large pan put the vegetable stock, thyme, half the hot pepper, half the onion, curry powder, black pepper, the trip and the trotters. Cook on a low heat until the meat becomes tender (about 35 - 40 minutes). Remove the meat from the stock. Do not throw away the stock, set aside for later use.

2 Heat the vegetable oil in a large cast-iron pan, and fry the trip and the trotters for 5 minutes. Add the reminder of the onion and the palm oil and continue to fry until the onion are transparent. Add the puree and the reserved stock and simmer for a further 25-30 minutes.

3 Wash the okra thoroughly, then grate or blend in a food processor until smooth. Heat the water in a pan and add the okra, cook for 10 - 15 minutes staring all the time to avoid the okra from boiling over. Season with salt.

Serve the okra in dip bowl with the trotter and trip stew on top and pounded yam.

Sweet Potato And Brown Beans

2 large sweet potatoes
2 cups brown beans
1 tbsp Palm oil
Water
Salt to taste

1 Wash the sweet potato and put on a greased baking tray. Roast the sweet potatoes in there skins at gas mark 4 for 1½ - 2 hours or until cooked through.

2 Wash the bean and put in a large pan, add enough water to cover. Simmer for 30- 40 minutes or until tender, adding more water when needed. Once all the water has evaporated add the palm oil and salt if needed and mix, set aside. Cut the sweet potatoes in half and serve with the beans on top.

Serve with any roasted meat such as chicken or beef on the side.

Note: *The brown beans used here cook very quickly and have a sweet taste so you don't need to soak them before hand.*

Eastern Africa

East African cuisine is rich with ingredients such as coconut, chickpeas, banana, lentils and sorghum. These ingredients and plenty more are used to make distinctive east African dishes.

Beef And Coconut Milk Stew (East Africa)

300g Beef cut into strips
5 tbsp vegetable oil
1 tsp black pepper
½ cup fresh coriander chopped
1 tsp Curry powder or turmeric
1 ½ cup Coconut milk
1 small red chilli
1 medium Onion chopped
4 garlic cloves
Salt to taste

1 Cut beef into thin strips, put in a large bowl and set aside. Using a mortar, pound the fresh coriander, turmeric, garlic and the chilli. Put this in a bowl and add the oil to make a marinade. Add the marinade to the beef, then add black pepper and mix, making sure to massage the marinade in to the beef with your hands. Leave the meat in the fridge to marinate for one hour.

2 Put the beef along with the marinade in a large heavy-based pan and fry on very low heat for 10 minutes. Add the coconut milk and salt to taste and simmer on very low heat for 30-40 minutes, or until the meat is tender. Stir from time to time to avoid burning and add water if the sauce is too thick. Serve with boiled rice.

Note: If you do not have a pestle and mortar, you can use a food processor or blender.

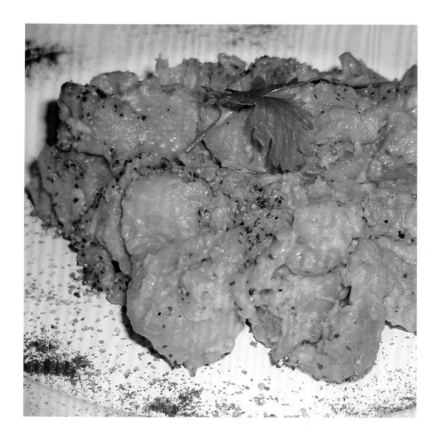

Chicken And Banana Stew (Tanzania)

600g. Chicken (Cut in pieces)
1 large onion finely chopped
3 small green bananas
2 tbsp tomato paste
2 tbsp tomato sauce
400ml coconut milk
100ml water
1 tsp curry powder
1 tsp salt
1 tsp black pepper
4 tbsp vegetable oil
2 garlic cloves crushed

1 Put the water into the pan, add the chopped chicken and boil for 20 minutes. Add the oil, chopped onion, crushed garlic, curry powder and black pepper, then cook for a further 5 minutes. Wash and peel the bananas and cut into thick round disks. Add these to the pan and cook for 5 minutes.

2 Add the coconut milk, salt, tomato paste and tomato sauce and simmer for 30 minutes, stirring from time to time to avoid burning. If sauce becomes too thick, add more water to thin. Serve hot with boiled rice.

Boiled Plantain With Chicken (Tanzania)

3 yellow plantain
600g. Chicken
1 medium tomato
1 medium onion
50ml vegetable oil
3 tbsp palm oil
1 tsp black pepper
150ml water
3 cloves garlic
1 stock cube
½ green pepper
1 small red chilli
1 tsp turmeric or curry powder
Salt to taste

A striking combination of moist, boiled plantain and fried chicken in a tomato sauce, served with boiled rice.

1 Leave the plantain in their skins and wash in cold water. Cut the plantain in half and put in a pan with water not quite covering. Simmer on very low heat until the plantain is tender (about 20-25 minutes). Remove the plantain and keep in a warm place.

2 Clean the chicken and cut into pieces. Put the chicken, 100ml water, stock cube curry powder, and black pepper into a pan and cook for 25-30 minutes, or until all the water has evaporated. Add the vegetable oil and fry the chicken for 20 minutes or until it is golden brown. Add the palm oil, stir and cook for 2 minutes, then blend the onion, garlic, 50ml water and tomatoes to a puree. Add to the pan with the chicken, add salt to taste and simmer for 20 minutes. Peel the plantain, add to the pan and cook on very low heat for a further 10 minutes. Serve hot with boiled rice.

Chicken In Coconut Cream (Tanzania)

400g chicken chopped
300ml coconut cream
2 tbsp grated coconut
toasted
1 medium onion chopped
4 tbsp vegetable oil
1 fresh chilli
4 cloves garlic cloves
crushed
1 tsp ground coriander
1 tsp finely chopped fresh
ginger
1 tsp curry powder or
turmeric
1 tsp black pepper
2 fresh tomatoes chopped
1 tbsp tomato paste
Salt to taste

1 Fry the chicken pieces in large heavy saucepan in the vegetable oil until light brown on all sides. Add the garlic and onions and fry until the onions are tender. Add the chopped fresh tomatoes, tomato paste, ginger, coriander and curry powder and simmer for 10 minutes or until the tomatoes are tender.

2 Add the coconut cream and black pepper and simmer for 20 minutes, stirring from time to time to avoid burning. Add the toasted coconut and serve with boiled rice.

Coconut And Broken Maize Pounding

2 cups broken maize (samp),
soaked overnight
¼ cup grated coconut
25g butter
5 tbsp sugar
400ml coconut milk

1 Drain and wash the broken maize, then put in a large heavy-based pan. Add enough water to cover and bring to the boil. Simmer for one hour or until the broken maize is tender. If water evaporates before it becomes tender, add more water and cook until the broken maize is very tender.

2 Once the maize is tender, drain and add the coconut milk, butter and sugar and mix thoroughly. Put the maize in a baking dish and finish with a topping of grated coconut, bake in a preheated oven at gas mark 4, 180°c for 25-30 minutes or until most of the coconut milk has evaporated and the top is light brown. Serve hot as a dessert.

Note: Dried broken sweet corn kernels can be used in place of the broken maize.

Okra And Chickpeas In Tomato Sauce

2 cups okra, thinly sliced
1 cup cooked chickpeas
¼ cup vegetable oil
2 medium fresh tomatoes
1 tbsp tomato sauce
1 tbsp tomato paste
1 small onion
2 garlic cloves, crushed
1 tsp ground coriander
1 tsp ground cumin
100ml vegetable stock
½ bell pepper
1 red chilli
Salt to taste

1 Heat the oil in a large, heavy-based pan. Add the chopped onion, garlic and bell pepper and fry until the onions are soft. Add the cumin and coriander and simmer for 5 minutes, then add the chopped tomatoes, tomato paste and tomato sauce and simmer for 10 minutes.

2 Add the okra and simmer for 8 minutes, then add the cooked chickpeas, stock and salt and simmer for a further 15-20 minutes.

Serve as a side dish or main meal.

Fish In Coconut Cream

2 fresh tilapia fish
200ml coconut cream
1 large onion
2 garlic cloves
1 large tomato
1 tbsp tomato paste
1 green chilli
½ green pepper
1 tsp curry powder
Salt to taste

1 Put chopped onion, green pepper and garlic in a pan and fry until tender. Add the tomatoes, tomato paste, chilli, curry powder and salt to taste. Simmer on low heat for 15 minutes or until tomatoes are tender. Add the coconut cream and simmer for a further 5 minutes.

2 Clean the fish, cut in half, add the fish to the sauce and simmer for a further 20-25 minutes stirring from time to time to avoid burning. Serve with boiled rice.

Chicken And Egg Stew (Ethiopia)

½ a chicken
2 teaspoons salt
1 large onion, chopped
½ red pepper
1 tsp black pepper
¼ cup vegetable oil
2 fresh tomatoes
2 tbsp tomato paste
1 garlic clove, crushed
1 tsp fresh ginger
Juice of two lemons
4 eggs
½ cup water
Salt to taste

1 Cut the chicken into pieces, place in a bowl and add salt, pepper and lemon juice. Leave the chicken to marinate for 30 minutes. Fry the onion in the vegetable oil in a heavy based pan until soft.

2 Meanwhile blend the red peppers, fresh tomatoes and hot chillies to a puree. Add the puree, tomato paste, crushed garlic, ginger and black pepper to the pan and cook on low heat for 10 minutes. Add the chicken pieces and water, mix well, then add salt to taste and simmer for 20-30 minutes. Boil and the eggs until firm, peel, then prick eggs with a fork once or twice and add to the sauce. Serve hot with boiled rice.

Broken Dried Maize With Spinach

(Tanzania)

1 cup fresh spinach chopped
finely
1 cup dried broken maize
(samp)
3 tbsp palm oil
1 small red chilli, chopped
¼ cup fresh coriander, chopped
1 tbsp tomato paste
½ small onion
1 tsp turmeric
Salt to taste

1 Clean and soak the maize overnight, drain then boil in a large saucepan until tender. Wash the spinach and cook in its own water until tender, set aside. Heat the oil in a saucepan, add the chopped onion and cook until transparent, about 5 minutes. Then add the tomato paste, turmeric and coriander and cook for one minute.

2 Add the cooked maize, spinach and chilli and mix thoroughly. Add salt to taste and serve as a main meal.

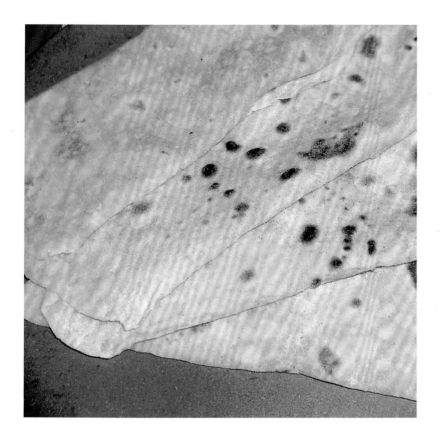

Chapatti (Tanzania)

3 cups plain flour
2 tbsp maize flour
1 tsp salt
6 tbsp oil
¼ cup hot boiling water

1 Sift the flour and salt in a bowl. Add oil and rub in until the mixture resembles fine breadcrumbs. Add the boiling water, a little at a time, and use a wooden spoon to mix the ingredients until you get a soft but not sticky dough. Leave the dough to cool, then knead for 10 minutes. The dough should be elastic.

2 Using your hand, make small balls. The balls should be small enough to fit in the palm of your hands. Roll the balls out on a floured board into large thin circles. Heat a large heavy-based pan and fry the chapattis on both sides until golden brown. Serve with a meat stew

Note: You do not need oil to fry the chapattis; all you need is a large heavy-based pan.

Minced Lamb Stew

500g minced lamb
1 large onion
1 large fresh tomato
3 garlic cloves, crushed
5 tbsp vegetable oil
1 cup tomato sauce
1 tsp hot chilli powder
1 large bell pepper
1 tsp curry powder
1 large potato, chopped
150ml vegetable stock
½ cup fresh parsley
Salt to taste

1 Saute the onion, bell peppers and garlic in 5 tablespoons of oil until they are transparent. Add the minced lamb and cook on low heat until the lamb is well browned. Add the chopped fresh tomatoes and simmer until the tomatoes are tender.

2 Peel the potatoes and cut into cubes, add to the lamb along with the curry powder, salt, the tomato sauce and the stock and simmer for 30-35 minutes or until the potatoes are cooked and the stew is thick. Add the chopped fresh parsley and chilli powder and cook for a further 10 minutes. Serve hot with boiled rice.

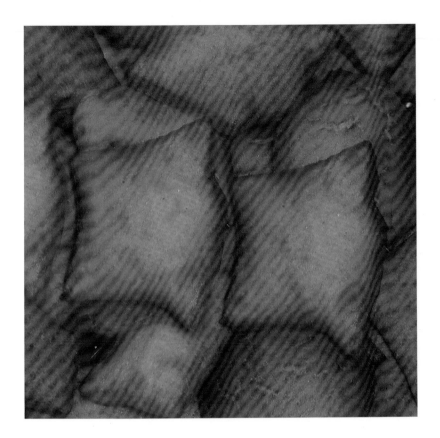

Mandazi, Maize Spicy Doughnut (Kenya)

100g maize meal
300g plain flour
½-tsp salt
4-tablespoon vegetable oil
1 tbsp fast rising yeast
1 tsp cardamom
70g sugar
150ml water
Oil for deep-frying

1 Sift the flour, maize meal and salt together in a large bowl, add the vegetable oil to the mixture, then add the sugar and the crushed cardamom seeds and mix well. Add the yeast, and then the water and mix to make a soft, but non-sticky dough. Knead the dough for 10 minutes.

2 Put the dough in a well-oiled bowl, cover and keep in a warm place overnight or until the dough has risen. Knead the dough and roll out flat, cut into small squares or other shapes and deep fry until golden brown.

Serve as a snack.

Injera Traditional Fermented Bread (Ethiopia)

250g millet flour
50g maize meal
1 tbsp fast raising yeast
½ tsp baking soda
1 tbsp sugar
½ tsp salt
650ml warm water

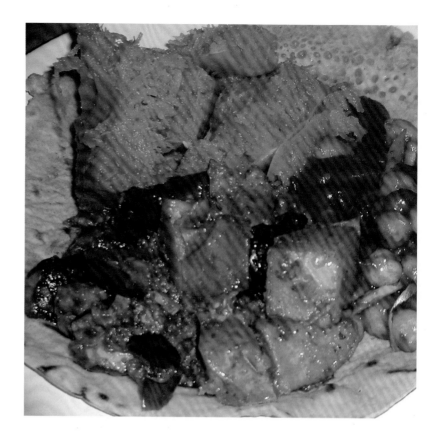

1 Mix the maize meal, millet, sugar and salt in a large bowl, then add the fast-raising yeast and the warm water to make a soft batter. Cover the bowl and leave in a warm place overnight. Add the soda to the batter and mix well.

2 Heat a heavy pan, then add enough butter to cover the bottom of the pan, swirl around and, use a tablespoon to spread to the edge of the pan, until you get an even coating. Cover and cook the injera on low heat until the bread is cooked. The bread should be firm to the touch and should look like a large crumpet with a lot of holes. Do this until all the batter is made into injera.

Serve injera on a plate with a meat and vegetable stew on top.

Lentil And Chickpea Dish (Ethiopia)

2 cups dried green lentils
1 cup chickpeas soaked over night
60ml vegetable oil
1 tsp salt
1 tbsp black pepper
1 tsp chilli powder
1 tsp curry powder
1 cup fresh parsley
2 fresh tomatoes chopped
2 tbsp tomatoes paste
1 large onion
1 clove garlic crushed

1 Wash the lentils in cold water, put into a large pan and add enough water to cover. Bring to the boil and simmer until the lentils are tender, then drain and set aside. Drain the chickpeas and put in another pan, add enough water to cover and bring to the boil, simmer until the chickpeas are tender. Drain and set aside.

2 Heat the oil in a in another pan, add the chopped onions and garlic and cook for 5 minutes. Add the curry powder, chilli, black pepper, tomato paste and fresh tomatoes and simmer for 10 minutes. Then add the chickpeas, lentils, vegetable stock, parsley and salt and simmer for a further 20 minutes. Serve as a main dish.

Spinach In Coconut Cream

4 cups fresh spinach, chopped
1 cup coconut cream
1 medium sized onion
2 medium tomatoes
1 tbsp tomato paste
Salt to taste
1 tsp curry powder
3 tbsp vegetable oil

1 Heat the oil in a large saucepan, add the chopped onions and fry until the onions are transparent. Add the chopped tomatoes, curry powder and tomato paste and cook for 5 minutes. Add the coconut cream and salt and simmer for 10 minutes.

2 Wash the spinach, drain and cut roughly, then add to the pan with the coconut sauce and simmer for 10 minutes, stirring from time to time to avoid burning. Serve with boiled rice.

Salt Fish Stew

200g Salt fish
1 stock cube
1 large potato
1 cup Spinach
3 garlic cloves
1 tbsp curry powder
1 large tomato
1 bell pepper
4 tbsp palm oil
1 green chilli
½ cup water
1 stock cube
1 large onion peeled and
chopped

1 Starting a day ahead by putting the cod in a bowl, cover the cod with cold water and soak for at least 12 hours, gently squeezing the cod dry and changing the water. Change the water at list 3 or 4 times.

2 Drain the cod, rinse it thoroughly under cold running water, and flake. Blend the tomatoes, pepper, garlic, curry powder, onion and chilli to make a puree, heat the palm oil in a heavy based pan and add the puree, then cook for 5 –8 minutes. Add the salt fish, potatoes, stock cube and water and cook for 20 – 25 minutes or until the potatoes are tender. Meanwhile wash the spinach and soak in hot water for 20 minutes. Drain and squeeze to remove the excess water, then add the spinach and cook for a further 10 minutes. Serve hot with Gari.

Note: salt fish contains a lot of salt so do not add more salt until you have finished cooking the dish. Taste first to see if more salt is needed.

Sorghum Cake

125g butter
6 tbsp sugar
3 eggs
180g plain flour
2 tsp baking powder
1 tsp nutmeg
4 tbsp sorghum flour
4 tbsp icing sugar
3 tbsp lemon juice

1 Cream the butter and the sugar until it is light and creamy. Beat the eggs and add a little at a time until all the eggs have been added. Sift the flour, nutmeg and the baking powder in a separate bowl, then add to the creamy mixture and mix thoroughly.

2 Put the mixture in a small, well-greased baking tin and bake in a preheated oven at gas mark 4, 180° C for 30-35 minutes or until the cake is golden brown and cooked through. To check if the cake is ready, pierce the middle with a clean knife and if it comes out clean then the cake is ready. Put the cake on wire rack to cool. In a clean bowl mix the icing sugar and lemon juice to make the icing. Once the cake is cool decorate the top of the cake with the icing as you please. Serve with tea.

Chicken and Lemon with Boiled Cassava.

Chicken & Lemon
400g chicken, chopped into pieces
10 fresh garlic cloves, peeled
1 large onion, cut into quarters
1 tsp ground black pepper
Juice of 3 large lemons
¼ cup vegetable oil
Salt to taste
½ cup water

Cassava
1 large fresh cassava root
Water
1 tsp salt
1 tsp coarse black pepper

1 In a large dish marinate the chicken with the onion, garlic, black pepper, salt lemon juice, water and 2 tablespoons oil. Mix well cover, put the chicken in the fridge and leave for 2 hours. Remove the chicken from the marinade, put the rest of the oil in a large heavy based pan and add the chicken. Fry the chicken until golden brown. Remove the onion and garlic from the marinade and add to the pan; fry for 5 minutes then add the rest of the marinade and simmer for 20-30 minutes.

2 Peel the cassava, cut in half and put in a large pan. Add 1 teaspoon salt and enough water to cover and bring to the boil. Simmer for 20-25 minutes or until the cassava is tender not mushy. Drain and cut cassava roughly with a knife, sprinkle with black pepper. Serve the boiled cassava with the chicken and lemon.

Note: Cassava skin can be tough, so use a small sharp knife to peel slowly and carefully and wash after you peel. It may also be very difficult to cut the cassava into small pieces before it is cooked, so boil first.

Boiled Samp And Chicken Stew

Boiled Samp
200g dried samp (broken dried maize)
100g fresh sweet corn kernels, boiled
50g boiled kidney beans
1 tbsp vegetable oil

Chicken Stew
2 Onions chopped
2 medium tomatoes chopped
1 tsp ground black pepper
Salt to taste
1 fresh chilli
½ of a whole Chicken chopped
1 cup fresh crawfish
3 tbsp palm oil
1 cup fresh Spinach
½ cup water
1 stock cube

1 Wash and boil the broken maize until it is tender. If using fresh corn on the cob, boil until corn is tender and then remove from cob with a knife. Wash and boil the kidney beans until tender and set aside. Mix these ingredients in one pan, add 1 tablespoon of vegetable oil and cook for 5 minutes. Keep in a warm place.

2 Cut the chicken into small pieces, add one teaspoon salt and one teaspoon black pepper. Mix thoroughly, then roast in oven until the chicken is evenly browned. Set aside in a warm place. Meanwhile soak the spinach in hot water for 10 minutes, drain and set aside. Blend the tomatoes, onions and chilli to make a puree. In another pan heat the palm oil, add the puree and cook for 10 minutes. Add the roasted chicken, spinach, crawfish, stock cube and water and cook for a further 20 minutes. Serve the broken maize, sweet corn and beans mixture on a plate with the chicken stew.

Index